"Women Mentoring Women for Momentum: The Next Step in Leading While Female *is a powerful and necessary call to action for women in educational leadership. The book speaks to my heart as a leader, a mentor, and a woman who has navigated the very barriers this book so clearly names.  The authors honor our journeys with honesty and courage, shedding light on systems that were not built for us while reminding us of the collective power we hold when we lift one another up. More importantly, it offers a path forward through intentional mentorship, sisterhood, and collective empowerment. The authors beautifully illustrate how women can build one another up, accelerate leadership growth, and create healthier, more equitable systems for the next generation. This is an essential read for anyone committed to cultivating courageous women leaders—and ensuring they not only rise, but thrive."*

Julie A. Vitale, Ph.D., Superintendent of Oceanside Unified School District

"Women Mentoring Women for Momentum: The Next Step in Leading While Female *elevates the impactful, tangible power mentoring provides in nurturing female leaders across educational sectors. As women lean into spaces that have often been inaccessible or arduous to enter, the authors artfully convey compelling experiences which are further grounded in research. This work is a gift to those in education and those who seek to lead in ways in and out of the classroom. As I read this work, I am reminiscent of my own female mentors who challenged me and gently prodded me to realize my own agency, helping me to spread my wings to seek and engage in leadership opportunities. As emerging female leaders navigate leadership opportunities, the role of female mentors serving in leadership roles proves invaluable as trusted supports who have encountered barriers and situations often unique to those leading while female. The authors illuminate those barriers women have encountered in attaining and sustaining leadership roles. This includes perceptions at the onset of applying for leadership positions, where implicit bias and stereotypes may cloud the belief that women can serve as leaders and excel in ensuring the successful implementation of district initiatives. The timeliness of this work reflects contemporary challenges where women serve as primary caretakers not just for their immediate family but for elderly parents while rising to meet the needs of their students and staff. In fact, the ability to support in multiple spaces and manage competing priorities highlight one of the greatest strengths of women in leadership positions."*

Mercedes Hubschmitt, Director II of UCSD Doctoral Program

*"The authors have done it again.* Women Mentoring Women for Momentum *is a powerful and timely addition to the Leading While Female series, offering both inspiration and practical guidance for aspiring and current female education administrators. Dr. Delores Lindsay, Dr. Trudy Arriaga, and Dr. Stacie Stanley illuminate the transformative impact of mentorship, weaving together research, personal stories, and actionable strategies that speak directly to the realities women face in leadership. This book is more than a resource—it's a call to action for women to lift one another, build confidence, and create lasting momentum in our schools and systems."*

**Dr. April Moore**, Superintendent at Sierra Sands Unified School District

*"Throughout my journey as a woman in leadership, I've been deeply influenced by the wisdom and generosity of women who led the way before me—mentors, colleagues, and dear friends who believed in me and helped me believe in myself. The authors of this book have been that to me. This book is both a call to action and a source of inspiration. It reminds us that mentorship is not a solitary act, but a shared responsibility—and that when women lift one another up and invest in each other's growth, we build unstoppable momentum."*

**Dr. Candace Singh**, Superintendent (Ret.), Fallbrook Union Elementary School District Leadership Consultant and Creator, AASA's Aspiring Superintendents Academy for Women Leaders

# Women Mentoring Women for Momentum

# Dedication

*I, Trudy, dedicate this book to my esteemed coauthors, valued mentors, and treasured friends, Stacie Stanley and Delores Lindsey. Our work to support women as leaders has resulted in deep and forever friendships with each other. I will always value our time around the Lindsey's kitchen table, with our relentless desire to support, lift, and promote educators who are* Leading While Female.

*I, Stacie, dedicate this book to my valued friends and mentors, Trudy and Delores. Through your mentoring, I continue to refine my craft as an educational leader. My hope is through our writing partnership and friendship, we have built something meaningful—a legacy of hope for the thousands of women leader voices we hear from as they seek to* Lead While Female.

*I, Delores, dedicate this book to my dear friends, coauthors, and mentors, Trudy and Stacie. Even though you did not know each other prior to our writing together, the three of us have become friends and colleagues. You are truly my mentors for creating the vision for* Women Mentoring Women for Momentum: The Next Step in Leading While Female

# Women Mentoring Women for Momentum

## The Next Step in Leading While Female

Trudy T. Arriaga

Stacie L. Stanley

Delores B. Lindsey

# CORWIN

FOR INFORMATION:

Corwin

A Sage Company

2455 Teller Road

Thousand Oaks, California 91320

(800) 233-9936

www.corwin.com

Sage Publications Ltd.

3rd Floor, HYLO

103-105 Bunhill Row

London EC1Y 8LZ

United Kingdom

Sage Publications India Pvt. Ltd.

10th Floor, Emaar Capital Tower 2

MG Road, Sikanderpur

Sector 26, Gurugram

Haryana - 122002

India

Sage Publications Asia-Pacific Pte. Ltd.

18 Cross Street #10-10/11/12

China Square Central

Singapore 048423

---

Vice President and Editorial
  Director:  Monica Eckman

Acquisitions Editor:  Megan Bedell

Content Development
  Editor:  Lucas Schleicher

Editorial Assistant:  Natalie A. Delpino

Project Editor:  Aparajita Srivastava

Copy Editor:  Michelle Ponce

Typesetter:  C&M Digitals (P) Ltd.

Proofreader:  Dennis Webb

Cover Designer:  Candice Harman



This book is printed on acid-free paper.

Printed in the United Kingdom
by Henry Ling Limited

26 27 28 29 30 10 9 8 7 6 5 4 3 2 1

# CONTENTS

# FOREWORD

In May 2020, during the pandemic, #MeToo, and Black Lives Matter movements, Trudy T. Arriaga, Stacie L. Stanley, and Delores B. Lindsey published the book that female educational leaders did not know they were waiting for, *Leading While Female: A Culturally Proficient Response for Gender Equity*. The authors of *Leading While Female* had started a private Facebook page. When I was invited, I then invited all the females I thought would want to be a part of the community. As we were in the early months of the pandemic at that point, I posted on that page, "We should have a book study." Dr. Delores Lindsey replied, "If you host it, we'll come." We planned for a four-Monday series, each night 1 hour and a half. I made a promotional flyer and promoted the book study for a month. By June 2020, we had over 500 educators sign up. I had to buy a bigger Zoom license, and the Leadership Book Chat was born. Close to 500 showed up. Those virtual meetings were full of connections, capacity building, and inspiration, in a time where so many felt isolated. With women attending across the United States, we found solidarity and validation on a national level. The *Leading While Female* Facebook group became a place for people to celebrate women's accomplishments, as well as their rising in educational positions. *Leading While Female* became a national movement and an annual conference. The first *Leading While Female* conference was virtual, held on a Saturday, with hundreds of women in attendance and purple *Leading While Female* t-shirts worn proudly. It became a hashtag: #LeadingWhileFemale.

Something magical was happening. Women who had never considered earning a doctorate began signing up for programs. Others who had never considered entering formal leadership started to apply. And others who had resigned themselves to working as assistant principals for their career, applied for principalships, and so on. Women, like myself, inspired by the authors, began writing the books, like the authors say, that "we wanted to read." Female educators were finding their voices. They were reaching out to each other for support outside of the book study. We witnessed a momentum of women claiming and taking up space. We saw more women of color rising. New educational #SisterCircles were being created across the nation. This is not by chance; this is by design.

In 2023, the authors gave us a way to reflect on our journeys in the *My Leading While Female Journey: A Guided Reflective Journal* asking all the right questions to assist us in being more reflective and intentional about our *Leading While Female* journey. The first in-person *Leading While Female* Conference happened in 2023. Although many women were connecting in spaces both virtual and in-person at this point, this was the first time we were coming together for a *Leading While Female* conference. The 2-day powerful experience grounded us in our why, journeys, and connections with one another.

The *Leading While Female* work is intentional work. In *Leading While Female: A Culturally Proficient Response for Gender Equity* Chapter 3 Confronting and Overcoming Barriers, we are charged with seeing *mentors as allies* and *supporting women educational leaders*. In *My Leading While Female Journey: A Guided Reflective Journal* the authors ask us to *reflect on having multiple mentors, ensuring that all leaders seeking executive leadership roles have a mentor who is mentoring us and who are mentoring others*. It is no surprise that *Mentoring for Momentum* is the next book. It is the piece that all need to engage in to keep moving women forward. In a profession that is dominated by women with females making up 87 percent of the profession, it is disproportional to have men make up 75 percent of the nation's superintendents. As educators, we are told to eliminate disproportionality in the data. *Women Mentoring Women for Momentum: The Next Step in Leading While Female* empowers us to do this.

In October 2024, the authors hosted the Leading While Female Conference in Minnesota. I had the privilege of attending, and it was incredible to be surrounded once again by so many women who have had their careers changed by the *Leading While Female* book and journal, as well as women who had not read the book yet. It was empowering to hear Minnesota superintendents and state leaders speak their truths about their journey. It was inspiring and galvanizing. I gained a sisterhood of educational leaders in Minnesota.

In 2020, with *Leading While Female*, we all gained three more mentors, sponsors, and coaches: Trudy T. Arriaga, Stacie L. Stanley, and Delores B. Lindsey. They have empowered us through their writing, speaking, and actions to do more and be more. Now they are empowering us to carry the torch to build the capacity of the next generation of female leaders to do the same, as well as this new generation of educators to know what to look for in a mentor, sponsor, and/or coach, to know the difference, what actions to take and questions to ask.

Now in 2025, we are seeing a pushback in society on the social, political, and economic gains made by women and people of color. We also see it specifically in education. During the pandemic, many women of color were hired as superintendents and several lost their jobs (Arundel, 2022; National Superintendents Roundtable, 2021). After many years of having a woman in education themed issue of a leadership magazine, in 2024 that theme was eliminated. After a decade of a region hosting a woman in leadership networking night, a man's voice was the loudest in an executive board meeting communicating that it wasn't necessary or fair that we continue the event, even though there were funds to support it. The networking event was eliminated. These are just a few examples and a microcosm of the pushback and momentum lost. This is not by chance, this is by design.

As I said of the other *Leading While Female* books, I wish this book would have existed earlier in my career. I am a firm believer in continuous growth and improvement for all, especially educators, so I am excited for all of you to have this guide to intentionally and explicitly "mentor with momentum." Lack of mentoring was reported as a major barrier by female leaders throughout the nation. This is a barrier we can control. We are in a time where we cannot wait. There is urgency around this work to be sure that we are coaching and being coached to create even greater equity, opportunities, access, and success for not only our children/students/scholars but also our staff, families, and communities. We will not go backward. We will only move forward. If the system was perfectly designed to get the results it gets, then let us design a new system to get new results, one designed in a matriarchal and familial way of mentoring.

The *Women Mentoring Women for Momentum: The Next Step in Leading While Female* book is exactly the book we need now. It is time and this is a call to action for all of us to sense the urgency and mentor with momentum.

—Renae Bryant, EdD.

Leader, adjunct professor, speaker, Your Story Matters podcast host, & *The Ed Branding Book* author "Your real job is that if you are free, you need to free somebody else. If you have some power, then your job is to empower somebody else."

—Toni Morrison

"I am no longer accepting the things I cannot change. I am changing the things I cannot accept."

—Angela Davis

"The most common way people give up their power is by thinking they don't have any."

—Alice Walker

"We can disagree and still love each other unless your disagreement is rooted in my oppression and denial of my humanity and right to exist."

—James Baldwin

"Freedom is never voluntarily given by the oppressor; it must be demanded by the oppressed."

—Dr. Martin Luther King Jr.

## REFERENCES

Arundel, Kara. (2022). *Superintendent turnover escalates, women still underrepresented.* K-12 Dive. https://www.k12dive.com/news/superintendent-turnover-increased-during-pandemic/638724/

National Superintendents Roundtable. (2021). *Superintendents struggle during pandemic: Panic attacks, strokes, & threats of violence meet prayer, exercise, meditation, and booze. A report from the National Superintendents Roundtable.* https://www.superintendentsforum.org/reports/report-superintendents-struggle-during-pandemic

# ACKNOWLEDGMENTS

We greatly appreciate the women leaders who participated in our inquiry study about barriers and support factors for mentees and mentors. We honor the women throughout the nation who are *Leading While Female* and took their precious time on behalf of other women to be a part of our study. We acknowledge the women who have blazed the trails and walked before us. We stand on your shoulders as we hand the baton to the next generation of female leaders. We give gratitude to the female superintendents of this nation. Your unique contributions are acknowledged, recognized, and appreciated. Because of you, young women and little girls who dream of leading, can look up and find themselves. If you can see it—you can indeed, be it!

We thank our families who support us and honor the work we do in our attempt to blend our personal and professional lives. Our husbands, Raymundo, David, and Randy are true feminists. They support, walk along side, assist, and celebrate our work. We recognize and appreciate your contributions, and for this, we offer gratitude and love.

As a writing team, we are deeply appreciative of the expertise and support of the Corwin team. Thank you to our editor, Megan Bedell, and the support team, Mia Rodriguez, Natalie Delpino, and Lucas Schneider. We continue to be grateful to Dan Alpert, who supported our work with his excellence and relentless advocacy prior to his retirement.

Thank you to the numerous authors who are cited in this book. We appreciate and acknowledge the work you have done before us to ensure equity and access for all leaders. We intentionally cited the first names of all contributing authors to ensure the female authors are highlighted and recognized.

Finally, we thank each other. We sang together in triumph and held each other up in times of hardship. We made it through and modeled the true meaning of mentoring for momentum.

## PUBLISHER'S ACKNOWLEDGMENTS

Corwin gratefully acknowledges the contributions of the following reviewers:

Angela M. Mosley, Ed.D.
Professor
Brightpoint Community College
Midlothian, VA

Brenda Lewis, Ph.D.
Superintendent of Schools
Fridley Public Schools
Fridley, MN

Dr. Elizabeth Alvarez
Educator
Forest Park D91
Forest Park, Illinois

Dr. Jacie Maslyk
Educational Consultant
Pittsburgh, PA

Jaguanana Lathan, Ed.D.
Chief Executive Officer/School Board Trustee
New Generation Equity®/Antioch Unified School District
Antioch, California

Lena Marie Rockwood
Assistant Principal
Revere High School
Revere, Massachusetts

Dr. Mandy Bell
Director of Elementary Education
Oceanside Unified School District
Oceanside, California

Margarita Cuizon-Armelino
Executive
Association of California School Administrators
Sacramento, California

Mayra Vega-Manríquez
Assistant Superintendent of Administrative Services
Ocean View School District
Oxnard, CA

Dr. Talisa Sullivan
Consultant/Educator
Transformational Leadership Consulting Services
Hemet, California

# ABOUT THE AUTHORS

**Dr. Trudy T. Arriaga** served the Ventura Unified School District for 14 years as the first female superintendent. She began her career as a trilingual paraeducator and enjoyed 40 years of service in education as a teacher, assistant principal, principal, director, superintendent, and university instructor at all levels.

Trudy retired as superintendent in July 2015 and was honored by the naming of the VUSD District Office, The VUSD Trudy Tuttle Arriaga Education Service Center. She is currently the Advisor for Educational Leadership and Partnerships at Cal Lutheran University. Trudy is the coauthor, with her esteemed colleague Dr. Randall B. Lindsey of *Opening Doors: An Implementation Template for Cultural Proficiency,* which delivers a compelling account on how leaders can create and expand cultures of inclusion and equity by dismantling and crafting new organizational policies and practices on behalf of the students they serve. Her second book, *Leading While Female: A Culturally Proficient Response to Gender Equity,* coauthored with Dr. Delores Lindsey and Dr. Stacie Stanley, offers a counter narrative and strategies to overcome the barriers of women in educational leadership, followed by the companion journal, *My Leading While Female Journal.* It has been her privilege to assist educational districts, institutions, and organizations throughout the United States through keynote speeches, workshops, leadership and equity institutes, and online professional development to align the actions of organizations with their stated values and principles in their effort to build a culturally proficient and inclusive organization for each and every one. Trudy and her husband, Raymundo, are enjoying this grand chapter of life as grandparents to Rayo Mana and Sofia Anuhea. Trudy can be contacted at trudyarriaga73@gmail.com.

**Dr. Stacie L. Stanley** currently serves as the superintendent of Saint Paul Public Schools (SPPS), the second largest school district in Minnesota. Prior to her appointment in SPPS, she served as the superintendent of Edina Public Schools. Stacie has served in a variety of education roles including math teacher, school principal, and director of curriculum, assessment and instruction, and prior to serving as superintendent, she served as the associate superintendent of Eden Prairie Schools. Dr. Stanley fervently believes that the "answer is in the room" and building leadership capacity through dignity supports organizational transformation.

Dr. Stanley earned a doctorate degree from Bethel University in Saint Paul, Minnesota, where she researched the impact of intercultural development on K-6 administrative leadership practice. She is a fierce advocate for creating safe spaces of belonging for each and every student that allow them to know their worth and thrive. Stacie is the coauthor of *Leading While Female: A Culturally Proficient Response for Gender Equity*. Dr. Stanley also served as a contributing author for the text *Innovative Voices in Education: Engaging Diverse Communities*.

Dr. Stanley is a doctoral program adjunct faculty member and advisor at Bethel University in Minnesota. Stacie lives in a multigenerational home with her husband and 95-year-old father and enjoys being an empty nester, power walking, and spending time with their grandchildren. Follow Dr. Stanley on instagram @DrStacieStanley or LinkedIn Stacie Stanley, EdD.

**Dr. Delores B. Lindsey** served as assistant principal, principal, and county office administrator. She served as executive director of the regional school leadership center. Delores uses her skills as cognitive coach and adaptive schools trainer blended with her understanding and skills as a cultural proficiency trainer to design and implement the 10-Day Certification Program for Culturally Proficient Educational Practice. She served as assistant professor at California State University San Marcos for more than 10 years. She retired from the institution; however, she has not retired from the education profession. Her primary focus is developing culturally proficient leaders. She helps educational leaders examine their organizations' policies and practices and their individual beliefs and values about cross-cultural communication. Her favorite reflective questions are, Who are we? and, Are we who we say we are? Delores and her husband, Randall (her favorite SAGE/ Corwin author), continue to co-write about the application of the four Tools of Cultural Proficiency. Her most recent publications, which are on Corwin's bestseller list, are *Leading While Female: A Culturally Proficient Response for Gender Equity*, and *My Leading While Female Journey: A Guided Reflective Journal* with Trudy Arriaga and Stacie Stanley.

# INTRODUCTION

*Before I walked on stage to present, a woman I did not know, quietly and gently fixed my collar and whispered, "I wanted you to look your best."*

Trudy Arriaga

## WHY WE WROTE THIS BOOK

One of our greatest strengths as women resides in our sisterhood with other women. This book is designed to guide women to mentor for momentum as we seek and become female mentors and mentees. We continue to identify a disproportionate number of females in roles that do not carry decision-making power within the profession that is labeled, the "women's profession." Our children are watching and waiting, and there is no time but the present to act in support of each other as women. Mentor programs are essential for the success of leaders and women gaining leadership positions (Burns, 2025). The literature suggests that women are less likely to have strong female leaders to guide them than their male counterparts. Lack of female mentors becomes an obstacle for women and puts them at a disadvantage in acquiring leadership positions. The "tapping on the shoulder" of women influences motivation to pursue leadership, gives women confidence, and serves as an entry into existing networks of women in leadership. Investing in women through capacity building, mentors can significantly enhance leadership potential. By prioritizing capacity building through mentorship, districts can enhance the leadership skills of women and contribute to long-term sustainability and career longevity (Burns, 2025).

As we researched the extensive and complicated realities of women who lead in our books, *Leading While Female: A Culturally Proficient Response to Gender Equity* (LWF) and *My Leading While Female Journey: A Guided Reflective Journal*, we set out to identify barriers that many women face as they strive to secure positions in educational leadership. The barriers are social constructs that function as negative core values that result in resistance to gender equity. We interviewed and interacted with female educators across the nation in our *Leading While Female* research, and if you were a reader, you may recall that we went into great depth to discover the most common barriers that women identified in their quest to move forward as educational leaders. The following are the eight barriers identified:

- Systems Not Made for Women
  - Elimination of job sharing, meetings going overtime in the late afternoons, lack of lactation stations, and biased family-friendly benefits are relatable and specific examples of systems not designed for working women with responsibilities outside of their professional lives. These examples of a lack of flexibility in the workplace resulted in gender pay inequities as the ultimate realities of systems that are not made for women. According to Maranto et al (2018), men are promoted after 10.7 years of teaching compared to women teaching an average of 13.2 years before taking leadership roles. Women also report that their perception is that school boards set higher expectations for female principals compared to male principals (Watson et al., 2017).

- Traditional Career Pathways
  - Women generally begin their careers as elementary teachers. If they move through the system, the pathway is often in curriculum and instruction with years of experience in positions such as the teacher on special assignment, curriculum coordinator for elementary education, and director of curriculum and instruction. This is not the pathway to the executive cabinet level and leads to longer and often unreachable career paths to the superintendency for women. The research substantiates secondary leaders have an advantage over elementary leaders in being selected for executive cabinet positions (Wallace, 2014).

- Traditional Interview Process
  - The interview process for administrative positions frequently revealed a process of embedded, unconscious gender bias. Women reported being questioned about their family commitments in the interview process (Sawchuk, 2022). Suggestions such as "this will be a big job" and questions like "who will take care of your children?" were articulated to the authors numerous times. The language in the advertisement of the positions, lack of diversity of the panel, questions asked, discussions following the interview by the panel, reference checking, and, ultimately, the process for the decision were all found to be laden with gender bias and often a resistance to a woman securing the position. Stories of critique of appearance such as the styling of hair, clothing, makeup, and even shoes

became subjects that often were coupled with women's experiences in the interview process. Research has shown that bias continues to exist in hiring practices. When women are successful in leadership positions, they are considered the exception (Burns, 2025).

▶ Cultural Norms and Dual Identities

- Unapologetically, we are women with multiple identities and not limited to grandmother, mother, wife, daughter, aunt, and superintendent. Balancing careers with home lives can be difficult and even impossible in organizations that do not recognize nor honor the dual roles of women who lead. Women reported facing bias and stereotypes about their leadership capabilities as well as their home and family responsibilities.

▶ Delays Along the Way

- Women reported delays along the way to achieving their next career steps. Delays included maternity leave, child rearing, care of elderly parents, and following their spouses to other communities for career advancement. These realities and responsibilities women face in their struggle to maintain their homes and family are recognized as barriers.

▶ Myths About Women's Qualifications

- *Women do not have business acumen . . . women are too soft . . . women do not have the courage.* We heard these quotes throughout our research and continue to hear them today. Our response is, *do not mistake our greatest strengths as weaknesses.* Women have reported hearing biased statements such as, *you are not proficient with budgets and the political aspects of the job yet,* and *we are not ready for a female superintendent yet* (Arriaga et al., 2020, p. 60). Women are often the *risky choice* or the *let's give her a shot* choice, when indeed they rise and achieve.

▶ Lack of Confidence . . . not Competence

- The profession said to be the women's profession continues to be led predominantly by men. Even though *nearly eight in 10 public school teachers are women,* men continue to fill the majority of leadership positions. Women are now the majority in educational leadership doctoral and master's programs. Yes, women prepare themselves well by earning master's and doctorates in education. The University of California at Los Angeles (UCLA, n.d.) reports that 66 percent of their students in educational leadership master's programs are women. Although women have prepared themselves well, many lack the confidence to apply for higher level positions.

- Lambert (2025) of California's EdSource publication reported that, nationally, 53 percent of state superintendents in 2025 are female, up from 47 percent last year. Women hold one-third of the district/school superintendent's jobs in the United States. Half of all superintendents appointed to the top job in the largest 100 school districts are women. Despite that, at the current pace of change, it will take almost 30 years before there are as many women serving as superintendents as men.

- The study reported that in the western United States, 37 percent of the superintendents are women—up from 30 percent last year. The highest percentage of female superintendents is in the northeastern part of the country, with 46 percent. The number decreased from 54 percent from last year. The southeast has the lowest percentage of female superintendents, with 22 percent.

- EdSource's report came from The ILO Group, a national education strategy and policy firm.

▸ Lack of Female Mentors

- Women reported that they have greatly benefitted from male mentors and colleagues, yet many indicated they have not had a female mentor. This supportive environment for women did not always exist, and thus, they did not have the opportunity of shared experiences, confidence building, and navigating challenges through the lens of another female. The lack of opportunity for assistance with addressing the barriers listed previously prevented them from having valuable insights into those who had similar experiences specific to gender barriers, including work-life balance, self-confidence, networking, and, ultimately, finding success and satisfaction in their professional and personal lives.

As we have traveled the country and continue to meet, greet, and gather with women who lead, the subject of lack of female mentoring became the recurring theme. We realized the final two barriers, lack of confidence and lack of female mentors, were not only related but are the two barriers that we as women can control. Thus, we set out to dive deeper into the realities and research of females mentoring females. Our research has uncovered the reality that securing female mentors directly impacts the confidence versus competence barrier. Building each other's confidence is a major focus of the mentoring process.

This book is not designed to disparage nor minimize the tremendous assistance we have received from our male colleagues as mentors throughout our journeys. Rather, this book is designed to clarify that female mentors can provide assistance, guidance, and support in ways that males cannot due to specific insights and experiences of female leader.

We encourage our readers to take advantage of the multiple best strategies on how to become a mentor or a mentee. Our research indicated that lack of time is the greatest barrier to seeking a mentor relationship. We have addressed possible strategies in Chapter 4 to find ways to free up time for mentoring. As sisters in leadership, we are here to support you to find time for yourself to mentor and be mentored.

We took some time to reflect on our own stories of mentoring and appreciate the opportunity to share our stories with you in this section. Perhaps you will find yourself in our stories and thus they will become our shared experiences.

## TRUDY'S MENTORING STORY

Randy, Rich, Joe, and Bob. I am so very thankful to the four most significant professional mentor colleagues in my career. Each one gave of their knowledge, resources, and connections. Each one believed in my ability to lead and my ability to make hard decisions in a soft and gentle way. Each one provided a sense of loyalty and comfort to me, yet were honest and direct with their feedback. I am forever grateful to four male allies, who became advocates. I could not have done the work that I did without their mentorship and certainly would not have enjoyed the level of success that I secured as an educator who was *Leading While Female.*

It does not go unnoticed that my mentors were all males. I had wonderful female friends, colleagues, mother, sisters, and daughters who supported my efforts, laughed with me in triumph, and cried with me in hardships, but I did not consider them to be my mentors. There were times when I desperately needed a female mentor. I would have benefitted from a successful female who was in the role or had successfully been in the role of superintendent. The opportunity to have had a female mentor to leverage mutual support and understanding would have been a tremendous asset in my growth as a female leader. The connections and opportunities of women who shared common identities, backgrounds, and experiences would have been so valuable in the times that I needed a female perspective. I am pleased to say that in the twilight of my career, I have found female mentors. Among my mentors are my two coauthors, Delores and Stacie. They are dear friends and treasured mentors at this point in my journey.

When I became a superintendent in 2001, I was forty-four years old and the first female superintendent in the history of the district. In the same year, 14 percent of the superintendents in the United States were females. I was in a league of my own in many meetings and forums. There were a few other female superintendents in my county, but I did not want to bother them as I knew they were busy with no time to spare. I recall my very first superintendent's conference. I went to the registration table, and the woman at the table took one look at me and informed me that that teacher conference was across the street. When I told her I was a superintendent, she apologized profusely and told me I was just not what she expected. When I entered the large conference room, there were over 100 men in the room and very few women. I sat at a table with all men, and finally one of them acknowledged me and began by saying I must be a superintendent/principal of a small school district. I could have used a female mentor at that moment!

I recall the time a male colleague sent me an email in all caps and bold exclamation marks and called me a "bitch" in the text. I was devastated and did not feel that my four mentors could relate to the impact of that text. I recall the time that I wore my dress inside out! Yes, as a superintendent, I was on a campus with my dress inside out. I was beyond humiliated when it was finally pointed out to me. How I wish I had a female mentor at that moment to assure me that it will be forgotten by next week. Or perhaps the time I had to give lay-off notices and went to every person individually and knew that this decision was harming their families and their well-being. I lost sleep and friends . . . but it was my job, and I was going to face each one of them personally. I would have loved to have called a female mentor as I drove home in tears.

I have had the pleasure and privilege of mentoring many women in my career. I am honored to be asked and value the mentoring relationships established, which eventually become friendships. Sometimes it is just taking the call, keeping the lunch date, sending the article, or providing assurance that this, too, shall pass. Other times it is strategically assisting with the master plan or the relationships with the Board of Trustees. The informal and the formal moments can be equally beneficial.

To my formal past and present mentees—Rebecca, Sherrill, Michelle, Mary, Sara—I will continue to watch and support you with incredible pride as you make your marks as female superintendents. To my informal mentees, I hope that I have been there when you needed me and cleared the pathway to success through my actions of deep respect and admiration for each of you. Carry on!

## STACIE'S MENTORING STORY

I've had quite a bit of time to reflect on my journey with mentoring. As I journaled about my experience with mentoring, I realized that early in my career it was random, at best. Given that mentoring is an approach that is designed to provide specific guidance to "develop leadership skills, increase self-confidence, improve emotional intelligence, and navigate gender-specific obstacles to career advancement" (Kramer, 2021). I had a few indirect opportunities for growth. For instance, as a teacher, I was tapped on the shoulder by a principal to join the site-based leadership team. While there were not one-to-one meetings scheduled to discuss how this opportunity would develop my leadership skills, that certainly happened. During my tenure, I learned to listen more than speak. I learned the true meaning of compromise, and I began to see myself as a "leader" in our school. The next tap came from my superintendent who asked me to sit on a strategic planning committee. He shared that this was because of my extensive experience on curriculum committees. Again, he did not share that he saw promise and wanted to mentor me for the succession of district office positions. Yet, through this opportunity, I broadened my networks and developed a foundational understanding for the "why" of a strategic plan and the importance of ongoing monitoring. This opportunity also placed me in front of hiring authorities who were able to observe my abilities. I will never forget the moment that I was pulled aside and told by a cabinet member with hiring authority that they were surprised I hadn't applied for a principal opening in the district. Wow, what a door opening experience *and* a confidence builder that allowed me to see myself beyond the informal leadership roles I had held up to that point.

Perhaps the tap that was the most life- and career-changing experience was when my assistant superintendent told me there was an opening for an assistant superintendent (a promotional opportunity) in Eden Prairie, MN, and wondered if I wanted her to put in a good word for me. Again, she had not officially mentored me to prepare for this role, and she modeled the importance of keeping an eye out for growth opportunities of the staff

I led even if it meant a replacement search. She also modeled the benefits of sponsorship. That tap led to what I see as the first formal mentor I had. My superintendent told me from the onset that he knew I was going to be a superintendent, and he wanted to make certain that I had the operations project management experiences I needed, including direct leadership in a bond referendum. He also helped me build networks with Rotary and the local Chamber. As I navigated experiences, he asked questions, provided mentor coaching, and truly prepared me for my first appointment as superintendent.

Ultimately, all those taps were meaningful and important and substantially prepared me along the way. In addition to building my skills in leadership development and systems management, increasing my self-assurance, and strengthening my emotional intelligence, the taps allowed me to build self-sufficiency and resilience. Each built confidence to move into positions with increasing influence and oversight. My formal mentorship experience intentionally prepared me for my first superintendency *and* my new position in a district where I now serve more than three times the number of students and families. My hope in sharing my journey is that readers will understand that the mentoring path may not always be direct or intentional, and yet with personal reflection and tenacity, women leaders will meet their career advancement goals.

## DELORES' MENTORING STORY

*I'm so sorry, Delores, but this assistant principal position is one for a man. He's the last one on campus in the evenings after events like sports events and community events. I just wouldn't be a gentleman if I asked you, a lady, to be the last one to lock up on campus at night. The next AP job, the one for curriculum and instruction, will be yours, I'm sure you understand.*

Do those words sound familiar? If you read our first book, *Leading While Female: A Culturally Proficient Response for Gender Equity,* then you recognize the words of my mentor, the principal of the high school where I had taught for several years. He was the first mentor I had, and he advised me to get my master's degree in educational leadership including my Principal's Certification and prepare myself to be a school administrator. He had always praised my teaching, school leadership, and community engagement. I had supervised many after-school and evening school activities that required me to be the last person on campus in the evening. So, I was caught by surprise when he said he could not select me for the assistant principal position because of my gender. Although he continued to

be my mentor for the next few years, our relationship was never quite
the same.

Following my move from Louisiana to California in the early 1980s, I realized
I needed a mentor to help me navigate along my new career path. I searched
for someone who knew the application of California Educational Code as well
as assessment, curriculum and instructional strategies that were different
for me. I was a bit surprised when I first found a network of female leaders
before I found that one mentor to guide me on my advanced leadership
path. The women's leadership network was informative and supportive for
my growth. I found myself relying on two female colleagues who held the
same position I did for 5 years. We three were assistant principals of middle
schools with male principals. Our relationship began when we met for early
morning coffee once a week to talk about things our jobs had in common.
As our relationship grew, we relied on each other for story sharing, lessons
learned, and emotional support. We became peer-to-peer mentors supporting
each other through personal and professional successes and challenges. The
formal relationship ended when one of our colleagues took a lateral position
in another district, one was promoted within the district, and I took a
principal's position in another district. We remained connected informally for
several more years, but our trio mentorship came to an end when our needs
had been met.

When I became principal, I reached out to the male who had been principal
when I was the assistant principal to be my mentor. I held such high respect
for how he aligned his leadership skills with the values he held for serving all
students. For the first time as an educator, I saw what it meant to publicly
state your values and beliefs about education and leadership. I was able to
engage in formal and informal conversations with him about, *Why do you do
what you do?*

Once again, I found the technical support I needed from a mentor as well as
the emotional support that comes from knowing the day-to-day challenges
and successes in the world of middle grade students and their families. He
remains my friend today even though our formal mentor relationship ended
when I left the principalship.

I found myself at my career crossroad once I had earned my PhD and had
served 6 years as middle grades principal. I had been on the career path to
be superintendent, when my dissertation chair, a former superintendent,
asked me, *"Given your skills as a professional developer and leader, what are*

*the reasons you want to be a superintendent? What might be an alternative path that is also attractive to you?"* I had never thought of these questions before. Now, what was I going to do?

My next step came because of a good friend's encouragement. She suggested I apply for an executive leadership position with a state leadership professional development organization. She was right to suggest that position would help me decide which road to take at my career crossroad. Once I engaged in my role of researching, developing, and implementing a statewide leadership program, the goal of superintendent was no longer my focus. As part of my new job, I became a member of a local five female member leadership team and gender mixed members of a statewide organization that sustained my growth for the next 5 years. This executive leadership role served as the transition role to becoming a tenure track faculty member at a state university campus. My good fortune led me to my mentor for all things higher education. She guided me from committee meetings through the feared tenure process. Although my time at the university ended, my friendship with my mentor continues.

My lessons learned have guided me to become a mentor to female mentees as they engage in their leadership journeys. I may be at the most enjoyable and rewarding point of my 50+ years career.

One of our greatest strengths as women resides in our sisterhood with other women. This book is designed to guide women to mentor for momentum as we seek and become female mentors and mentees. Mentoring for momentum is purposeful and intentional mentoring. It is a dynamic and supportive relationship that propels women to ensure that we do not lose ground. Together, we will partner to build confidence, gain skills, and accelerate our move forward as women who lead.

We have identified numerous barriers as we continue to promote our unique contributions as women who lead. Let us not create our own barriers! It is heartening to see over 2,300 people on our *Leading While Female* Facebook page! Women in leadership networks are popping up across the nation, and the formation of sister circles is bringing women closer together in sisterhood! Now is the time to mentor for momentum.

# CHAPTER 1

# FINDING OUR MOMENTUM

*A true mentor helps you find your own voice and strength.*

— Unknown



**Administrative Coordinator: Induction, Credentialing, & Contracts**

Office of the Chief Human Resources Officer

Division of Human Resources

*I have mentored emerging female leaders as part of our Doctoral Program for over 10 years. I've found a constant clash exists between my female candidates and their male supervisors' authoritarian leadership approaches. The emerging female leaders' styles, which often are more collaborative, community building, and relationship-based than their male mentors' are, simply looked down upon by their male supervisors. It seems some men view these women as "idealist" and "ineffective" leaders. Many of the emerging female leaders see male leaders in their higher positions as role models and emulate these behaviors. Sometimes the advice women hear is, as a woman leader, you don't have time for that.*

*The top-down approach is seen as a necessary trait for administrators. I have seen females' ideas blatantly shut down, dismissed, and ignored. Seems I see it most often with male leaders of color as they work with females of color. The patriarchy patterns are often repeated unless they are interrupted. Female leaders have typically conformed to the male-dominated system or challenged it. Conformity is viewed as a strong, intimidating force. Even when women present an alternate approach to resolve an issue, they risk being seen as insubordinate. Often, when a female leader engages in the discussion and presents an appropriate or innovative response, she is ignored or criticized. As mentor to these emerging female leaders, I offer breakthrough, mediational questions to help them think about what it will take to overcome the barriers of "we've always done it this way."*

Delina's story is one example of the value of coaching within a mentoring relationship. As you think of mentoring relationships you have experienced, in what ways have coaching skills informed the mentee's pathway to a new job? And secondly, in what ways has the absence of coaching skills served as a barrier for you as mentee or mentor?

_______________________________________________________________

_______________________________________________________________

_______________________________________________________________

_______________________________________________________________

## THREE THINGS FOR YOU, OUR READER COLLEAGUES

The following are the intended goals of this book:

- ▸ First, this book presents and values the importance of educational leaders serving as formal or informal mentors and/or role models for emerging female leaders. The authors define and apply the Tools of Cultural Proficiency to provide momentum in narrowing and closing the gender equity gap.

- ▸ Second, this book shares related research emphasizing the importance of women mentoring women leaders, survey data illustrating barriers for female mentees and mentors, and female executive leaders' stories from women mentoring women.

- ▸ Third, this book offers a pathway for emerging leaders (mentees) to locate and utilize the guidance of mentors.

This is a stand-alone book, or it can be used as a companion workbook/ guide for *Leading While Female* and *My Leading While Female Journey*. The content is a continuation of review of related research and of storytelling to provide readers opportunities to record their personal experiences of being mentored, providing guidance to others, and serving, in turn, as role models for colleagues just beginning their journeys in leadership. In each chapter, we share stories of female mentors as examples of formal, informal, and peer-to-peer mentor relationships. Using their support factors to overcome barriers, mentors guide their mentees forward in their career paths.

## Delina's Mentoring and Coaching With Ashanti

As we learned earlier, Delina mentors emerging female leaders engaged in their doctoral programs. She relies on coaching skills when her mentees are faced with gender equity issues in the program or in their organizations. Recently, Delina met with her mentee, Ashanti, director of instruction at a local district. Ashanti is a rising star in her district and is on target to complete her doctorate this year. She is one of a few women of color candidates in the program and is well-prepared to compete for assistant superintendent positions available in the area this spring. She contacted Delina to meet with her about a situation that occurred in a class session:

**Delina:** *I'm glad you stopped by Ashanti. One of your friends told me about what happened in Dr. Alfred's seminar session. I wanted to hear from you. Tell me what you want me to know.*

**Ashanti:** *Oh, Dr. Lopez, I'm so upset! I can't believe he said that. We were having a class discussion about current issues in education and how different local district leaders were responding to these issues. Mark Peters said something about it seems there are more female superintendents in this area than ever before, and he asked Dr. Alfred if that is a good thing or not. Dr. Alfred said, 'Well, Mark, it seems we have more problems these days, so what do you think? Are those two things related?' Then he chuckled and smirked. None of the women laughed. Then, he looked at me and asked, 'So Ashanti, why do you think there more female executive leaders now than we had 5 years ago?' I said in my most confident voice, 'Dr. Alfred, are you really asking, can women do the job? Women have always been qualified, but they've faced more challenges than their male counterparts. Now, the whole system is changing. It's no longer the good ole boys club. In my district, women are being seen as highly qualified candidates. He looked at me and said, 'Maybe we all need to do more research on this question.' Then, he dismissed class. Am I wrong Dr. Lopez?*

**Delina:** *First, let's talk about how that question and response made you feel.*

*Ashanti described how demeaned she felt and added she felt Dr. Alfred was demeaning all female leaders.*

*Delina paraphrased Ashanti's comments and continued to listen as she explained they had never talked about the challenges women leaders faced in becoming leaders compared to how quickly men in the program had gotten leadership roles. Ashanti shared how the women often met after seminar to talk about similar challenges they were facing. Then, Delina asked Ashanti mediational (breakthrough) questions designed to help her mentee assess her cultural knowledge and manage the inequities of the gender gap.*

**Delina:** *Ashanti, as you think of the gender gap that has existed in this country, what are some ways you and the other females in the seminar could demonstrate the need for understanding the inequities of the gender gap? What might be some ways for the organization's members to understand the advantages for female leadership in organizations?*

Ashanti looked at Delina with wide open eyes and a smile on her face: *That's it! I hadn't thought about that. I'll get back to you and let you know how it goes. Thank you, Dr. Lopez.*

Delina was confident her mentee would engage other females in the seminar in thinking about ways to manage the diverse views in the class.

## Reflection

What were some things you noticed about Delina that makes her a culturally proficient mentor?

_____________________________________________

_____________________________________________

_____________________________________________

_____________________________________________

Over time, effective mentors leave their mentees with practical, actionable leadership skills they can use in any future professional pursuits. Leadership topics covered within the mentee-mentor relationship include, but are not limited to, effective communications, conflict resolution, decision-making, problem resolution, managing organizational culture, building trust, and developing diverse and inclusive environments. Additionally, the mentee and mentor develop a reciprocal relationship built on trust and confidentiality. Mentors share lessons learned along the way with their mentee while the mentee has opportunities to ask questions that might feel too risky in other work-related situations.

As sustained growth and relationship development require more than a one-*and-done experience*, we maintain well-developed mentor programs with planned events, and post-event follow-up sessions have offered critical turning points in mentees' careers. Mentor programs have provided networks of personal and professional support and given mentees the confidence they need to apply, interview, and take on new leadership roles. In Chapter 5, we provide details for designing and implementing highly effective, equitable mentor programs.

## Equity Tools for Support

As self-identified equity warriors, we believe current organization systems too often have suppressed women's opportunities at all levels. We find systemic oppression of women and people of color continues to exist and persist in school districts and other organizations where women work to achieve the same leadership levels as their male counterparts. As a part of the United States' history, traditions, and economic status, many white men have enjoyed power in the form of privilege and entitlement, as in legacy access to leadership roles. Certainly, we are not suggesting white men haven't worked hard for what they have, as we have all heard. However, too often, white men are not fully aware of their power because they have never experienced the absence of it (Delpit, 1988).

We offer the Tools of Cultural Proficiency to guide the mentor in planning meaningful, intentional conversations with her mentee. The stories are examples of how female mentors bring support to their mentees to be aware of this system of privilege and entitlement and develop skills to work toward a culturally proficient response for gender equity. In combination, the Tools of Cultural Proficiency—Overcoming the Barriers, the Guiding Principles, the Continuum, and the Essential Elements (Lindsey et al., 2019)—provide a framework for analyzing her beliefs and values and behaviors as a mentor. Once she has an awareness of who she is (actions aligned with beliefs and values), a mentor intends for the relationship with her mentee to be reciprocal and culturally responsive. The mentor and mentee are aware of the Tools of Cultural Proficiency and the importance of leadership practices to overcome barriers toward gender equity. The Tools are further defined in

Chapter 3, and the importance and benefit of the tools are explored further in each subsequent chapter.

## TERMS IN CONTEXT

We employ and describe a variety of terms to support and enhance your learning about establishing equitable mentoring programs, creating pathways for gender equity in the workplace, and for developing culturally proficient practices in support of colleagues who are *Leading While Female.*

The following terms are defined in the context of this book using the lens of cultural proficiency:

*Belonging:* The feeling of security and support along with a sense of acceptance, inclusion, and identity. Belonging is not about fitting in but about being accepted, loved, and respected for who you are. When one feels included and connected, she can flourish without fear of judgment.

*Diversity:* Unique differences, including but not limited to gender, ethnicity, race, language, religion, faith, age, sexual orientation, disability, socioeconomic status, physical and mental ability, and cultural backgrounds.

*Equity:* Fairness and justice of treatment of women and men according to their respective needs. Individuals may need different supports to achieve similar outcomes. All individuals do not start from the same place; therefore, effort must be made to acknowledge and adjust for imbalances that impede or block pathways to leadership. Opportunity is not limited simply on the basis of gender. Correcting for gender biases, however, ensures outcomes improve for all.

*Inclusion:* Vision and practice of welcoming, valuing, and supporting people across varying identities so they feel represented and heard. In an inclusive environment, people feel they fully belong, are authentic, can contribute to the collective, have a voice, and fully participate in a diverse society.

*Inquiry:* Author collected data from participant interviews and surveys used in this book.

*Sponsoring:* Often a senior employee in the workplace invested in the growth and career progression of an employee, the boss, the leader of an adjacent business unit, or even a C-suite executive. Sponsors are advocates, endorsers, and champions of another's professional trajectory. Sponsors often take an active role in colleagues' advancement by identifying high-potential individuals and providing them with stretch assignments or high-visibility projects. Some risks may be involved in sponsorships if the employee does not perform well.

We have noticed the words *coaching* and *mentoring* are sometimes used as if they are interchangeable. However, each word has its own definition. Here's how we define and use these important terms:

***Coaching:*** One person mediates the thinking and behavior of another person by asking mediational (thinking) questions. The mentor as coach is reflective and mediational, not advising.

***Culturally Proficient Coaching:*** Intends for the person being coached to be aware of the cultural connections within the community they serve and to be culturally responsive to the diverse needs of individuals and organization members.

***Culturally Proficient Mentoring:*** Intends for the relationship with her mentee to be reciprocal and culturally responsive. The mentor and mentee are aware of Tools of Cultural Proficiency and the importance of leadership practices to overcome barriers toward gender equity.

***Mentoring:*** A learning relationship focused on long-term career development for the mentee. The primary purposes of mentoring are to drive personal growth and to build leadership skills, knowledge, and understanding. Mentors may use coaching skills in their conversations; however, the mentor role is wider than that of a coach and may include opening doors, making connections, and sharing experiences (Leadership Alliance, 2024). The relationship between mentee and mentor is reciprocal. Both the mentor and mentee may benefit from the relationship. Given the hierarchal nature of supervision of employees, it is recommended a person's manager is not her mentor.

***Reverse Mentoring:*** One individual considered younger shares knowledge, experience, and skills in a specific area with someone who is less knowledgeable, more senior, older, and/or typically less experienced. For example, this method of mentoring can improve diversity and inclusion cultures in an organization as a junior member educates a senior member about the challenges she faces as a member of the LGBTQAI+ community that the senior member may not be aware or truly understand. Reverse mentoring is a powerful model for school leaders to consider tapping into for improved communication and a broader sense of inclusivity.

***Role Modeling:*** A person whose behavior as a leader in a particular role is imitated by others. An educational leader behaves in ways other educators admire and wish to emulate.

## Reflections

Given the Terms in Context used in this book, what stands out for you?

___________________________________________________________

___________________________________________________________

___________________________________________________________

___________________________________________________________

Which of the terms would you like to explore more in depth, and why?

___________________________________________________________

___________________________________________________________

___________________________________________________________

___________________________________________________________

As you review the list, what term (or terms) is missing? What else would you like to know more about within the context of this book?

___________________________________________________________

___________________________________________________________

___________________________________________________________

___________________________________________________________

## What's the Relationship Between Coaching and Mentoring?

The learning relationship between mentee and mentor requires both members to be focused on the career development of the mentee. Ideally, reciprocal mentorship is a broad, outcomes-based relationship requiring mentee and mentor to be nonjudgmental and aware of long-term career growth for mentee and mentor. While the central goal of the relationship is focused on the mentee, the mentor benefits from assessing cultural knowledge of the mentee, demonstrating the value she holds for the mentee, and learning to manage and adapt to the dynamics of difference arising from discrepant experiences of gender, ethnic, racial, and social class membership. The mentor learns to guide conversations based on needs of the mentee and searches for resources to enhance and improve the career path of the mentee.

Coaching occurs within the context of the mentor's role in response to concerns about equitable access opportunities and continued professional advancement. For example, a mentor builds a long-term relationship focused on the mentee's goals for career advancement. Within that context, the mentor uses culturally proficient coaching skills to help mediate the mentee assessing her cultural knowledge as an interview candidate. Let's suppose the mentee, a high school principal, schedules an appointment with her mentor to talk about an upcoming interview for director of secondary instruction. The mentor is a role model for emerging leaders in the district. Her leadership inspires the mentee and other emerging leaders. The mentor uses her coaching skills to mediate the principal from her current role to the desired role of director. The principal and her mentor are aware she is the only candidate of color in the interview process. The mentor listens closely for the principal's values and beliefs aligned with the vision of the district. Her coaching questions focus on her mentee's cultural knowledge of self and the organization. The mentor also benefits from the conversations, developing her coaching skills and maturity as a mentor. The reciprocal relationship the mentee and mentor develop ensures a greater possibility for each to grow and reach her professional goals.

**Exhibit 1.0** depicts the relationship between mentoring and coaching. Notice the "big picture" or long-term relationship of mentoring is sustained by coaching conversations over time. The mentor uses the breakthrough questions protocol to mediate the mentee's best thinking about her career path.

As illustrated in Exhibit 1.0, coaching is part of mentoring; however, mentoring may not involve a coaching conversation, depending on the skills of the mentor. Mentoring and coaching may stand alone as leadership skills; yet, when the skills are joined together, the relationship of mentee and mentor is enhanced, and the career development for the mentee is improved.

**Exhibit 1.0** • *The Relationship Between Mentoring and Coaching*

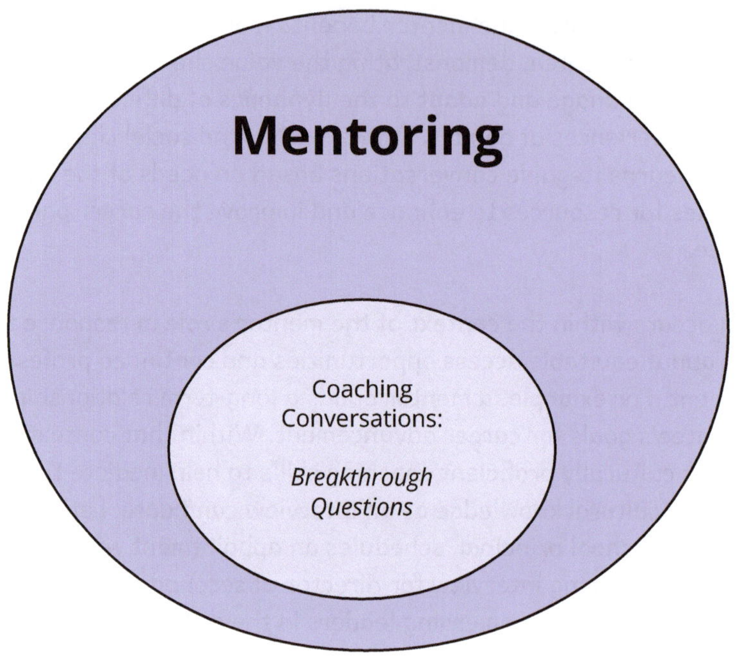


As shown in Exhibit 1.1, the combination of a culturally proficient mentor using coaching skills guides her mentee along her path to become a culturally proficient leader.

**Exhibit 1.1** • *Role of Mentor*

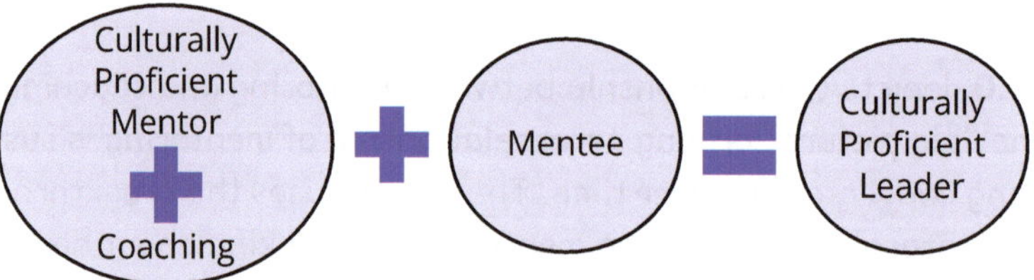


## A Word About Sponsors

As observed in Exhibit 1.2, mentorships involve two people, the mentee and mentor; whereas sponsorships must involve a third person. A sponsor is asking someone to think about or see their mentee differently.

**Exhibit 1.2 •** *Role of Sponsor*

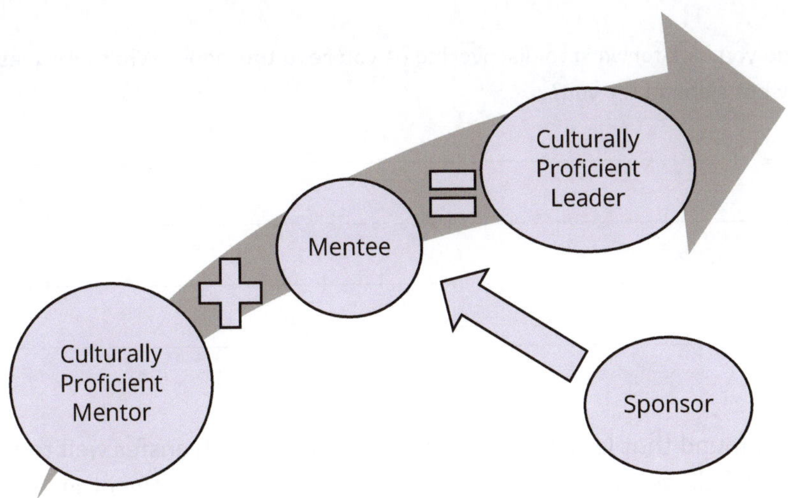


An effective sponsor presents the mentee with evidence for success to guide the mentee on her career path. The sponsor might also provide direct connections and opportunities for next steps. The performance evidence is more meaningful and requires fewer risks than a recommendation based on potential. An equity-minded sponsor is not necessarily a person of power but a leader mindful of the importance of representation, equity, diversity, and inclusion of leaders of color keeping performance evidence in mind. We have more to say about sponsorships in Chapter 5.

## Reflections

As presented at the opening, this book can be used as a companion to *Leading While Female: A Culturally Proficient Response for Gender Equity* or can serve as a stand-alone book. As you think of the triple goals of the book, in what ways do they resonate with you and your interests in the mentee/mentor's relationships?

_______________________________________________________________

_______________________________________________________________

_______________________________________________________________

_______________________________________________________________

*(Continued)*

(Continued)

What do you look forward to discovering as you read this book? What intrigues you about what's ahead for you?

___________________________________________

___________________________________________

___________________________________________

___________________________________________

We have found that lessons from the corporate world transfer well to the education field as you will see throughout the book. Our momentum builds as we explore more about forming equitable relationships in Chapters 2 and 3. We found mentors have expressed needs for self-care. Chapter 4 provides answers to many questions about making time for self. Chapter 5 describes roles and responsibilities of mentors and growing your own mentoring programs. Momentum increases as we detail the relationship between coaching and mentoring in Chapter 6. Chapter 7 offers additional strategies and our closing thoughts. And now, Chapter 2 shares the importance and strength of affinity groups.

Here is something to think about:

What are some things you're noticing about the relationship between mentee and mentor? And sponsor?

___________________________________________

___________________________________________

___________________________________________

___________________________________________

___________________________________________

___________________________________________

# CHAPTER 2

# GROUPS FOR GOOD

*A mentor is someone who allows you to see the hope inside yourself.*

Oprah Winfrey

As we mentor for momentum, we find that the strengths and influence of our female colleagues, networks, and mentors are undeniable. We benefit personally and professionally from spaces of vulnerability, commonality, differences, and understanding as we gather with other females. Women's affinity groups are not for sharing grievances or the woes of being a female who leads but rather a momentum to break through, lift up, and double down. From the affinity groups, we identify support from other women that often leads to mentoring, sponsoring, and coaching. Affinity groups are critical but not sufficient. Women continue to need the commitment of their male allies and advocates. The stated values of the organization must align with the actions to combat gender inequities and promote gender parity.

Affinity groups have been used for centuries to ensure that marginalized groups were able to come together to discuss issues of importance in a safe place. Throughout the United States' protracted era of slavery, individuals gathered to rally about areas of oppression, methods of escape, and ways to take care of those who would be left behind. The dawning of the 20th century saw women-led rallies. They gathered to speak about their concerns regarding the lack of protections provided due to a prohibition of voting rights. The ability to gather a contingency of women throughout the United States led to a sense of empowerment and, ultimately, advocacy and action that led to opening doors for women's voices to be present as they cast their ballots.

The first known workplace affinity group was reported to occur at Xerox circa 1970. The internal organization was formed to focus on the barriers to promotions, equal pay, and a lack of psychological safety that Black employees experienced at the time (Malone, 2022). Since then, affinity groups have organized across industries to support many groups, including the development and advancement of women leaders. Affinity groups provide a space for women educational leaders and those in the pipeline to analyze, discuss, and make sense of their workplace experiences that live across various stages of the continuum of cultural proficiency (Arriaga et al., 2020). The AASA national superintendent's organization launched the Women Educators Leading Learning (#AASAWELL) that provides training in areas of Leading For Equitable Outcomes, Financial WELLness, and Being Well to Lead Well.

The recent AASA survey of superintendents demonstrates that these spaces of affinity are still needed with just over 24 percent of superintendents nationwide identifying as female (Grogan & Nash, 2021). This statistic continues to be noteworthy given that 77 percent of teachers in the United States are women, a statistic that has remained steady for several decades. In addition, a deeper look into the cohort of women superintendents shows that just 1 percent of the cohort identify as Black (The Education Trust, 2023), 3 percent as Latinx, and very small numbers for those of the Asian and Indigenous heritage. In a recent study conducted by the authors, participants of color stated that supportive spaces with their colleagues help them develop the stamina to strategically navigate the many micro- and macro-aggressions they experience daily.

## PSYCHOLOGICAL SAFETY

Members of nondominant groups in the workplace are often positioned in environments where their creative ideas are minimized, or worse yet, credited to their less senior male peers. This is taxing and has an influence on productivity and job sustainability. Affinity groups provide spaces of psychological safety where female leaders feel comfortable speaking up or being vulnerable without the anxiety of wondering what it might mean in the context of their day-to-day work or opportunities for advancement. This moves participants from simply feeling *integrated* within an environment to feeling *included* (Cobb & Knownapple, 2019). Similarly, LeaderFactor (2025) names inclusion safety as the first stage of psychological safety: a person has a true sense of acceptance, trust, and belonging. These key components serve as the foundation for personal growth and development within the group. As trust grows amongst group members, so does courage. Courage to lean in more deeply into areas of personal growth, courage to take a risk and seek feedback, and courage to remain curious. Ultimately, a healthy environment of interdependence is cultivated, leading to greater confidence and workplace success and preparation for the next levels of leadership.

Professional development that occurs in women in leadership affinity groups aligns with skills and knowledge that have not typically been cultivated with females. For instance, as the authors work with women leaders, an area that consistently arises is the differences in communication patterns of men and women in the work setting. Women leaders often share about being talked over, feeling silenced, and at times, ignored. They speak about male peers taking credit for work that they have completed and frustration in not knowing how to respond. Rarely do organizations offer training about communication in their general menus of development, and all the rarer is professional development designed to support the skill development of female leaders specifically. Affinity groups provide the opportunity to experience an inside-out reflective process that helps women understand their ways of communicating, the connections to how women have been implicitly and explicitly nurtured to engage in small and large groups, and how those patterns may be helping and hindering their success. Finally, affinity group members are equipped and empowered to use this targeted learning as they continue to develop their leadership prowess.

Even in the context of affinity groups, it is important to understand the unique difference in needs that intersectionality brings to the space. As an example, the unique needs of women who are of Asian descent must be addressed and acknowledged in the context of that membership. Without this happening, stereotypes and microaggressions may be unintentionally perpetuated, leading to harm and disillusionment. Affinity group modeling allows for learner safety with the group and prepares members to transfer the knowledge as they work to advocate for others in their work environments.

> **We've all heard the saying *it's lonely at the top*. For female executives this colloquialism is often exacerbated. Women in the C-suite report high levels of isolation. Many times, she is the only female on their team and at times may be leading a predominantly male cabinet. Females may find themselves being more frequently questioned about their vision for the organization or decisions they've made. Female leaders of color report more targeted complaints to their superiors. These situations have an impact on mental health and can take a toll on physical health as well. Affinity spaces allow for these common experiences to be recognized, acknowledged, and for the barrier of isolation to be minimized. (ThomasFisk, 2024)**

## Vignette

*Breaking Confidence Confirmation: When Affinity Finds You*

*Jenae is an aspiring C-suite leader. She transferred from another state where she served in a variety of pipeline and pathway roles including executive director of business operations. Due to her need to return to her home state to care for her mother, she accepted a position as director of facilities. At the time, she understood that the position was a step back in her quest for a cabinet level position and figured she would have an opportunity to be promoted into a role more aligned with her expertise once she had more exposure in the district. Serving in a male dominated role has been more trying in her current context than she anticipated. Although she dealt with hostile and benevolent sexism when she initially broke into the area of business operations, she had proven herself and built strong networks in her prior district. After a year in her new district, she's experienced the early career tensions of the past. It has been hard to escape the barrier of the good old boys' culture, and she is yearning for affirming networks that will help her both grow as a leader and develop a cadre of sponsors.*

*A recent invitation to attend an affinity group for women educational leaders in the male dominated area of operations has been a gift. During her first meeting she was relieved to be in a room where she immediately felt accepted, valued, and quite honestly honored for her knowledge and expertise in her field. Since joining the district, she had developed the habit of explaining her experience to validate her credibility; she immediately realized that this wasn't needed in this affinity community. Her affinity group has provided a space of safety as she shared about the many microaggressions she has experienced, including consistent questioning and resistance to the efficiency protocols she has attempted to onboard in the organization. Some of the resistance included aggressive encounters about her so-called "girly" strategies.*

*During today's meeting, the facilitator offered a unique experience. There were breakout circles that supported deeper affinity—circles by race, gender identity, and industry. As a Black woman, Jenae gladly joined the affinity circle for women of color. During the circle dialogue, Jenae heard colleagues speak to experiences specific to those she has endured. One leader expressed the fatigue from having to be two times better than both their white women and men counterparts. Unlike their personal experience, males in their organizations—even direct reports—were presumed to be competent and skilled when they onboarded.*

*Members of the group provided additional resources and information about a local critical friends group for women leaders of color. She learned about a national sister-circle specifically for women of color and felt an immediate sense of worthiness when a colleague promptly added her and others to the group distribution list. She was delighted to exchange contact information with several leaders. She left feeling invigorated and relieved to know there was a light at the end of the tunnel. She was now connected and found a sense of belonging.*

A Guiding Principle of Cultural Proficiency asserts that individuals are as diverse within groups as between groups. While women have experienced oppression in the workplace for generations, the experience of women of color is more nuanced. Thought leaders and researchers such as Kimberle Crenshaw (2016) have long informed us about intersectionality or the dual impact that women of color experience in their career journey and especially as they move into executive leadership roles in fields dominated by men. The affinity group leaders in this vignette demonstrated exemplary responsiveness, as they not only created a welcoming space for women, they also understood that female leadership is complex and requires us to more comprehensively assess the cultural needs of all members. As Jenae shared, she found a space of belonging and connectedness.

## AFFINITY, MOMENTUM, SUSTAINABILITY

The support that comes with networking cannot be undersold. These communities of confidence empower women as their concerns are confirmed, and they can tap one another for strategies to navigate the situations they are experiencing. An added benefit is that the collegial relationships that are built often grow into long-term formal mentorships that prepare those entry-level leaders for movement in the pipeline toward executive roles. These same mentors may have influential connections in organizations, positioning them to sponsor the leader for an internship, apprenticeship, or open executive position.

Educational leaders are faced with many challenges, including funding shortages, increased mental health needs with staff and students, and staffing shortages. Leveraging the expertise, experience, and connection of members can lead to better workplaces and greater value of the education profession. Affinity group advocacy can have a significant impact on the success of the students and communities they serve. For instance, tied to staffing shortages is the continued need to diversify teaching ranks. Knowing that 77 percent of the educators in the classroom are female, advocacy in this area serves as a win–win; increasing pathways to teaching and bolstering pipelines to leadership for women of color.

So how does a district get started with supporting women through affinity groups? The answer is do just that—start. Here are some tips to get started:

- ▶ Assess the cultural knowledge of your organization. What is the experience of your Indigenous/First Nation female leaders? Who is visible, and who isn't?

- ▶ Look for programs in organizations that are successful, and model your group after their successes. Speak with members of the affinity group. What is it about that group that keeps them motivated to return?

- Encourage the creation of sister-circles, where the goal is to establish deep sister-like bonds. Female leaders come together to provide a community where it is safe to be vulnerable and share their trials and triumphs. Through relationships, they learn from one another, celebrating their gifts, and offering critical feedback for situations at hand. Members determine meeting frequency, location, and, if they desire, whether to have a single facilitator or if many circle members will guide dialogue and discussion.

- Market toward specific groups of women for registration. This means doing more than just sending out a flier or an email. There are times that women may feel hesitant to join the group because of the perception of it being an *affirmative action* promo. Speaking with female leaders directly and sharing the outcomes and benefits of attending, signing on may feel less intimidating.

- Understand that affinity groups are designed to be multimodal: provide a milieu for networking and resilience, engaging in brainstorming around barriers, and building skills and knowledge to *overcome* the barriers.

This chapter started with a mention of the women's suffrage movement. It was numbers and ultimately connections that got the vote for the amendment. Even with the enactment of the 19th amendment in 1919, women of color were not afforded the right to vote. Even with women advancing to close the leadership gap, women of color must continue to work together with their white collegial counterparts to narrow the gender *and* racial gap.

## Reflection

How might your organization's current culture either support or hinder the development of productive affinity groups, and what specific steps could you take to create psychological safety within these spaces?

_______________________________________________

_______________________________________________

_______________________________________________

_______________________________________________

_______________________________________________

Consider the intersection of your various identities (gender, race, professional role, etc.). How might an affinity group address your unique needs while also helping you develop as a more effective advocate for others in your workplace?

_______________________________________________

_______________________________________________

_______________________________________________

_______________________________________________

_______________________________________________

Chapter 3 provides a framework for developing equitable relationships and maintaining reciprocal responsibilities.

# CHAPTER 3

# EQUITABLE MENTORING MATTERS

*If you want something, dream, dare, do it. If you want something extraordinary, dream, dare, do it with great mentors. If you want to learn a powerful lesson about yourself, become a mentor.*

Shirley Liu

This chapter is an on-ramp guiding your journey as equitable mentees and mentors. This intended journey using The Tools of Cultural Proficiency benefits you professionally and, by extension, your colleagues, your students, and the community you serve. Cultural Proficiency is a framework for understanding how to interact effectively with people from other cultures or who are in a variety of ways different from ourselves. As important, this framework provides individuals with a way to examine their values, beliefs, and assumptions about how to react to those differences. Members of organizations use the framework to examine policies and practices aligned with their stated vision, values, and core beliefs. These close personal and organizational examination processes are the inside-out commitments to equity work. (Lindsey et al., 2020). In other words, *are we who we say we are?*

## PLANNED REDUNDANCY

Our intention is to present the Cultural Proficiency Framework in numerous layers of information and examples to enhance the mentor's learning of the power and impact of using the tools. A culturally proficient mentor uses Cultural Proficiency as a lens to examine her beliefs, values, and behaviors. For example, she models for her mentee developing a network of mentors for support, aka a sister circle. The culturally proficient mentor shares her mind-changing, breakthrough questions protocol with her mentee during coaching conversations focused on her mentee's career path and developing their relationship. The mentor knows the value of using the five Essential Elements as action words in the breakthrough questions, so her mentee does her own action thinking. For example, the mentor might ask her mentee the following question:

> *As you think of where you see yourself in 3 years, what might be some things you imagine will cause you to adapt your career based on your beliefs and values for serving all students?*

The mentee will give time to adapting her career path based on her values and beliefs. This kind of thinking leads to action. Let's examine the four tools again and see why they lead to action steps for equity.

## The Four Tools for Equitable Action

For purposes of review, the Cultural Proficiency Framework presents four powerful tools. When taken together, they provide mentors a foundation of values-based behaviors for successfully guiding and supporting relationships in diverse environments. Culturally proficient mentors view diverse cultures, languages, abilities, and sexual orientations as assets rather than deficits or problems to be solved. The following are the four tools:

- **The Barriers:** Social constructs that function as default core values that inhibit equitable access and opportunities for historically marginalized cultural groups. When understood, these social constructs assist in overcoming resistance to change

- **The Guiding Principles:** Underlying positive core values of the equity approach

- **The Continuum:** Language that describes both healthy and nonproductive policies, practices, and individual values and behaviors

- **The Essential Elements:** Behavioral standards for measuring and planning for growth toward cultural proficiency (Lindsey et al., 2019).

Knowing and understanding these tools prepares the mentor to act in ways aligned with her deeply held values and beliefs and that often unknowingly guide inside-out actions like decision-making and problem-solving. She guides her mentee to reflect and examine her own behaviors aligned with her core expressed values, beliefs, and assumptions. A close examination of each tool prepares the mentor for her culturally proficient educational behaviors.

## Applying the Four Tools

Overcoming Barriers to Equitable Mentoring

Historical and systemic barriers to equitable mentoring must be identified and described as ways that inform a mentor's growth. As we noted in Arriaga et al. (2020), these barriers are both individual and institutional barriers. The interaction mentors face can be categorized as these four barriers:

- Mentor is unaware of the existence of sexism and gender inequities as examples of systemic oppression.

- Mentor denies the current assignment of male leaders is part of embedded system of privilege and entitlement that favors White, male leaders.

- Mentor sees no need to change the way things are, especially in areas of recruiting, hiring, and retention.

- Mentor is unwilling to adapt to changing needs of community by having female (women of color, LGBTQ+, and White) candidates.

Equitable, inclusive, and diverse behaviors are often difficult to explain and live because of the imbalance of how the educational system is infused with the historical oppression of some groups and, at the same time, with the unearned and often unrecognized privileges and entitlement of other groups that are present into today's social inequities across society. Absent the knowledge and understanding of these historical implications for today's organizations and institutions, mentors may be at a loss to explain why some things get in the way of all students learning or some teachers believing they can educate all learners. These institutions and personal barriers are described here:

- **Barrier:** Absent equitable mentoring, the school and community systems will continue practices that often, unknowingly, oppress some and lift others. For example, some students are placed in low expectations/low performing classes, irrespective of actual grades, because of the demographic group with which they identify. While at the same time, other students are placed in high expectations/high performing sections because of their favorable group identity.

- **Barrier:** Our communities grow and change, yet without equitable mentoring, some leaders aren't aware they need to grow and change, too. For example, communities may change because of the influx of a different demographic group that lives in the area.

However, educators continue to teach in the same way without making necessary changes to meet the needs of the changing population.

- **Barrier:** Without equitable mentoring, some leaders believe staying the same is easier than growing and changing. For example, change and growth in a community may require educators to learn new and different ways to educate all learners. However, some educators will resist doing so, merely because change of any kind is viewed as unfavorable.

## Using the Guiding Principles to Counter the Barriers

As a counter measure to systemic barriers, The Guiding Principles of Cultural Proficiency provide ways for mentors to probe their own core values as they work with individuals who are different from themselves. The Guiding Principles help the mentor

- Know the reasons they are an equitable leader and mentor

- Be aware of their levels of cultural knowledge and the cultures represented in their community

- Know and understand the different and historical treatment of those cultural groups least well served in schools and organizations

- Know that those they mentor are individuals and members of a larger cultural group

- Know, recognize, and value the differences within cultural communities of their mentees

- Know and respect the unique cultural needs their mentees have

- Know the mentees they serve may define families differently and see families as the primary support for students

- Know and recognize the person they mentor may have experienced the bicultural reality for cultural groups historically underserved or not well served in our schools

- Know, adjust, and accept cross-cultural interactions as necessary social and professional communication dynamics

Leaders who know their personal "why" are equipped to guide their schools and school districts in articulating and living the "institutional why" stated in their vision and mission.

## Using the Continuum for Assessing Growth

The Continuum provides language for differentiating unhealthy, unproductive language from healthy, productive language (Lindsey et al., 2020). Understanding the Continuum allows the mentor to hear her own underlying assumptions as well as the assumptions of her mentee. The skilled mentor assesses the language of the mentee and determines questions to ask to help shift the thinking from where the person is to where she wants to be. Using the Continuum as an illustration, the mentor hears an embedded low expectations assumption in her mentee's words, *The kids from the trailer park won't be able to do the work of the new standards.*

The mentor asks a breakthrough question, *In what ways might you work with others on the leadership team to support the families from the trailer park area to be better prepared to achieve the new standards?* This question is designed to shift the mentee's thinking from *they can't* to *we can.* Use of the Continuum provides the mentor with a way to assess the mentee's growth toward culturally proficient leadership practice.

**Table 3.0** illustrates the power of seeing culturally proficient behaviors of a mentor (right side). The left side of the Continuum describes unhealthy, destructive, incapacitating, and avoidance behaviors.

**Table 3.0** displays how the Continuum is used for an individual and organizational assessment of work in progress. The Continuum is *not* intended to imply judgement or indict individuals; rather, it is for reflection and assessment of growth over time. This tool is informed by the Barriers on the left side and the Guiding Principles on the right side of the Continuum.

The six points of the Continuum for a mentor are described as follows:

- **Cultural Destructiveness**: Mentor seeks to discourage and eliminate women as leaders.

- **Cultural Incapacity**: Mentor seeks to make the culture of others, especially women and women and men of color, appear to be wrong and expresses no need for women leaders.

- **Cultural Blindness or Avoidance**: Mentor intentionally or unintentionally fails to acknowledge the culture of others, especially women and women and men of color. Gender blindness ensures traditional, male-dominated educational leadership roles continue.

**Table 3.0** • *Continuum for Culturally Proficient Mentoring: Assessing for the Extent to Which the Mentor Values, Manages, and Adapts to Culturally Proficient Practices*

| Cultural Destructiveness | Cultural Incapacity | Cultural Blindness (Avoidance) | Cultural Precompetence | Cultural Competence | Cultural Proficiency |
|---|---|---|---|---|---|
| Mentor **disregards** aspects and importance of race, cultural self-identity and mentee's gender, culture, or languages.<br><br>Mentor is unaware and/or fearful of acknowledging any aspects of mentee's race, gender, sexual orientation, culture, or home language. | Mentor **ignores** reference to her own or others' race, cultural, gender, and sexual orientation perspectives and/or encourages behaviors to assimilate to expected roles of the organization.<br><br>Mentor is aware of mentee's gender, sexual orientation but **expects** mentee **to assimilate** to be successful as a school leader. | Mentor **avoids** understanding race, cultural, and sexual identity to promote leaders.<br><br>Mentor **avoids guiding** mentee to manage unpopular decisions with dominant cultures, anticipate criticism, or accept personal and professional consequences for advocating for underserved communities. | Mentor **seeks input** from affinity groups but may not do so consistently from across all cultural groups.<br><br>Mentor **includes input** from a few members of one cultural group and assumes it applies to all members of that group. | Mentor is clear and comfortable about her racial, cultural, and sexual identity and **expresses value** of her mentee's racial, cultural, and sexual identity.<br><br>Mentor uses her position **to inform network members** about the needs of members of the LGBTQIA+ community.<br><br>Mentor **facilitates** an understanding of **changing** the nature of the service paradigm from equality to equity and works toward closing gender gaps. | Mentor **inspires her mentee** through her practice and wisdom of moral purpose for **equity for all**. Her mentee is rewarded through the **development of goals** and action steps, which enhance multiple perceptions, credibility, trust, and effectiveness in meeting the needs of the community she serves.<br><br>Mentor **embraces risk and criticism** as necessary on their leadership journey and guides her mentee in experiencing the value of risk taking as lifetime agents for equity and social justice. |

- **Cultural Precompetence**: Mentor is aware of what she doesn't know about working in settings with women as nonforrmal leaders or as formal, designated leaders. This is the initial level of awareness after which a person/organization can move in a positive, constructive direction. Mentors notice contributions of women leaders.

- **Cultural Competence**: Mentors view one's personal and organizational work as an interactive arrangement in which the educator enters diverse settings in a manner that is valued and additive to cultures that are different from the mentor, especially women and women and men of color. The Five Essential Elements are the standards for action to intentionally move forward with purposeful outcomes for gender equity.

- **Cultural Proficiency**: Mentors make the commitment to lifelong learning for the purpose of being increasingly effective in serving the educational needs of *all* cultural groups. Cultural Proficiency requires individuals and core leader groups to hold the vision of what can be; then, mentors must commit to systemwide monitoring and measuring (benchmarking) for success on the journey to gender equity.

The Continuum measures the extent to which equitable actions are taken. Specifically, the Culturally Proficient Mentor takes five actions identified as The Essential Elements.

## Using the Essential Elements as Action for Equity

The Essential Elements for Cultural Proficiency provide mentors with clearly defined behaviors to guide their actions.

The Essential Elements for mentors' equitable actions are as follows:

- **Assessing cultural knowledge:** Equitable mentors know their own cultural stories and are open to hearing the cultural story of the person they are mentoring. Also, mentors know and understand the culture of their organization and the impact it has on people of different cultural groups. Mentors establish outcomes and goals for growth.

- **Valuing diversity:** Equitable mentors demonstrate value for diversity through daily behaviors of respect and inclusion of multiple voices and perspectives.

- **Managing the dynamics of differences:** Equitable mentors know that conflict is natural and normal behavior within organizations. They know, understand, and demonstrate effective strategies for recognizing, addressing, and resolving conflict.

- **Adapting to diversity:** Equitable mentors develop skills for cross-cultural communication. They establish ways for groups to welcome and interact positively with newcomers, particularly those whose cultures may be new to the leadership community in the school or district.

- **Institutionalizing cultural knowledge:** Equitable mentors are skillful in using narrative inquiry research to tell the organization's cultural proficiency story. Mentors share professional learning strategies for leaders to know and understand the importance of culturally proficient leadership practice. Mentors assess growth over time and determine new outcomes and goals.

The five verbs—assess, value, manage, adapt, and institutionalize—are key action behaviors for mentors' beliefs, values, and assumptions about *Leading While Female*.

## Putting the Tools Together

Used in combination, these four Tools of Cultural Proficiency help mentors interact with their mentees. Since it would be impossible for any one person to know the characteristics and behaviors of all cultural groups, we advocate for mentors knowing differences do exist and those differences influence how people are seen, heard, and experienced by others. These differences naturally surface conflict, mistrust, resistance, and growth as learning about each other occurs. Culturally Proficient mentors establish ways that demonstrate high value for learning about the diverse behaviors, languages, beliefs, and perspectives in the community to resolve these conflicts, confront issues of mistrust, and, thus, overcome systemic barriers.

## Inequality in Early Years

How did we get here? From the time children start school, they encounter gendered expectations about boys and girls "good" or "should be" behaviors. These different expectations, as well as external pressure to conform to stereotypes about gender roles, "steer" girls and boys into classes and extracurricular activities, college majors and ultimately career directions. Steering leads to "occupational segregation," which is a major factor behind the pay gap: male-dominated jobs pay better than traditionally female-dominated jobs, even when they require the same level of training and skill (AAUW, n.d.). Therefore, equitable mentors are needed to open doors and escort more women through the leadership doors that have been traditionally closed.

## From Glass Ceiling to Broken Rung

Metaphors of invisible barriers for women in the workplace continue to exist since the *glass ceiling* of the early 1980-1990s when more women than ever were entering the American workforce. Even in the 21st century, it is common knowledge that progress has been steady but still slower for women compared to their male counterparts at executive level positions. Another invisible metaphor depicting slow growth for the female leader is *the broken rung* (Ellingrud et al., 2024). Imagine for a moment trying to reach the top of a ladder when the first rung breaks and the next steps are extra difficult to reach. Without reaching that first leadership promotion because of the barriers we mentioned earlier, women lose momentum before they ever get started. That's why mentoring, networking, and sponsoring are critical steps for increasing experience capital.

## The Tools Lead to Equitable Mentoring Programs

The Tools of Cultural Proficiency provide mentors a valued way of thinking of equity, justice, and a sense of belonging. The lens of Cultural Proficiency is a metaphor for examining our day-to-day actions (Lindsey et al., 2020). It is not enough to profess, "I'm an equitable mentor." The question is, "Am I who I say I am?" Do my actions match my stated values? Will a mentee be surprised at my behavior, or will she understand why I do what I do?

The questions that follow are to guide you and your colleagues as you design and implement mentor programs in support of schools, districts, or other educational organizations to serve at least two functions:

- ▸ Create an environment in which emerging and new leaders experience their cultural backgrounds being embraced as assets

- ▸ Provides an unabashedly proud public setting focused on raising all students to high levels because of, not despite, their cultural identities

Aspiring to and living equitable and inclusive behaviors are often challenging to organizations and their individual members. Our society is slowly, steadily, and often unevenly acknowledging the residue of historical inequities that persists within society and is evident when examining the demographic membership of most school organizations. Our experience is school organizations that express value for inclusion and live into that inclusion benefit from those experiences. Our hope is mentors will demonstrate these values as they are *Leading While Female*.

As you read the following questions, think deeply about your responses. The questions are designed to help deepen your thinking using the four tools:

What barriers get in your way?

- To what extent are colleagues encouraged to assume nonformal and formal mentoring roles?

  _______________________________________________________

  _______________________________________________________

  To what degree are mentoring roles equitably represented across cultural groups in your school or district?

  _______________________________________________________

  _______________________________________________________

**Guiding Principles**

  To what extent does your school or district have lived core values that engage educators in working with mentors who are culturally different from one another?

  _______________________________________________________

  _______________________________________________________

**Continuum**

In what ways would mentors from your school or district describe how diverse cultural groups are valued in your school or district?

_______________________________________________________

_______________________________________________________

In what ways might mentors convey negative messages or positive messages?

_______________________________________________________

_______________________________________________________

In what ways do the school or district recognize progress across cultural groups?

_______________________________________________________

_______________________________________________________

**Essential Elements**

In a recent meeting at your school or district, the discussion centered on mentors and their mentees. In what ways did the discussion provide opportunities for one's culture to be viewed as an asset in serving the academic and social needs of the school or district's diverse community?

_______________________________________________________

_______________________________________________________

_______________________________________________________

_______________________________________________________

## Now That I Know What I Know

Your work in this chapter helped surface barriers that get in your way of being an equitable mentor. Now, you are asking what are your next steps? Knowing The Tools of Cultural Proficiency and the ways in which they provide a foundation on which to build your actions for equitable mentoring, you are prepared to support mentee relationships grounded in equitable values for a safe and trusting environment.

### Reflections

As you reflect on your thoughts from this chapter, in what ways do The Tools of Cultural Proficiency inform your role as mentee or mentor?

___________________________________________________

___________________________________________________

___________________________________________________

___________________________________________________

What might be a barrier you will confront to become a more skillful mentor?

___________________________________________________

___________________________________________________

___________________________________________________

___________________________________________________

Many female leaders expressed the lack of time to pursue the next academic degree, or apply for the next level leadership position, or serve as a mentor. How do female leaders find time to be a mentor or a mentee? As female leaders seek to find more time, one way is for mentors to prioritize and blend the time they have in their personal and professional lives. Chapter 4 addresses many of these concerns and approaches for blending time.

# CHAPTER 4

# PERSONAL AND PROFESSIONAL BLENDING

*I wish I had treasured the doing it a little more and the getting it done a little less.*

Anna Quindlen

This chapter focuses on the stated barrier of the absence of time to be in a mentoring relationship. May we learn to prioritize and treasure the time spent with less focus on what did not get done.

## From Trudy

*The Anna Quindlen quote brought back a flood of memories of my mother's final years. She lived to be 101. Anna Quindlen was one of her favorite authors. When my mother turned 90, she made a bucket list of birthday wishes for her family to consider filling. Her birthday bucket list focused on passing time with the ones she loved. On her list were a glass of wine on the beach at sunset, a family gathering with no "electronics," a quiet chat in front of a fireplace, a drive up the coast to see the California poppies in bloom, a foot rub accompanied by long conversation and a signed copy of Anna Quindlen's book,* Lots of Candles and Plenty of Cake. *We managed to check off every wish on her list, and I now realize that each checkoff was a gift* to *us, not* from *us. She knew and understood the priority of time in her final decade of life on earth. She taught us well.*

## TIME, OR THE LACK OF IT

As we surveyed and spoke with women in leadership roles across the nation, the number one reason for not participating in a mentee/mentor relationship was time constraints. Because we only have 24 hours in a day, and that cannot be changed, it serves us well to pause and realign our priorities, our usage of time, and balance. A successful mentorship relationship that involves building strong connections must be one that allows for ample and allotted time between the mentee and the mentor.

If mentoring is indeed a priority to the mentor and the mentee, it becomes important to focus on the impact of the relationship. Rather than ask, "Do I have time to be mentored?" ask yourself if you have time not to be mentored. Will the missed opportunity result in missing the mark on my continued growth, objectives, and outcomes? If we only participate in our mentoring relationship when we have the time, we are likely not to give the relationship what we deserve. How do we free space and time to benefit from a mentor/ mentee relationship?

Great mentors are in high demand, especially female mentors and women leaders of color. As others seek guidance, the mentor begins to experience greater demands than she has time. If it becomes overwhelming or unmanageable, she may have to limit her one-one mentoring and provide small group seminars, informal mentoring, sister circles of influence, or recruit others to join her as a mentor. Informal and formal mentoring can serve as leverage for addressing equity, inclusion, and diversity. Mentor programs that are intentionally equity focused and designed with women of color in mind to address race, gender, and intersectionality may be able to create a critical pathway to leadership for Black and Brown women. The suggested models would be strengthened using The Cultural Proficiency Framework to embed institutional support, collective empowerment, acknowledgment of lived experiences, and affinity groups.

The expression of lack of time from women is not a new phenomenon. Musical song lyrics of today consistently remind women of the barriers of time that we experience as we unapologetically lead and prioritize and balance our personal and professional lives. Dolly Parton's *Working 9 to 5* reminded us that it was enough to keep us crazy if we let it, and most recently, Taylor Swift reminds us of running twice as fast and working twice as hard to keep up, in her hit song, *The Man*. The 50s reminded us of simply turning around and finding that time has passed us by in Harry Belafonte's song, *Turn Around*. The 60s reminded us of the value of time by The Pozo-Seco Singers with the lyrics of their song *Time: "Time, oh time where did you go? Time, oh good, good time where did you go?"*

Yes, we struggle to find time for our own well-being as we manage work and personal commitments. Taking time for ourselves can often lead to guilt or that overwhelming feeling of letting others down and not being enough.

## TO PAY OR NOT TO PAY?

Mentoring comes in all forms. There is no one-size-fits-all approach to mentoring. Formal, informal, teams, sister circles, reverse, and organizational are a few of the numerous possibilities of mentoring programs. Thus, there is no one answer to whether mentors should be paid for their time, expertise, and guidance. In the educational setting, generally there are only a few in the organization who have individual negotiated contracts. A superintendent will often negotiate the access to a formal mentor into their contract for the first few years. This is generally a paid position and one that assures the superintendent that they will have access to a seasoned mentor of their choice on a regular basis with expertise very specific to the unique role of the superintendent. This is an agreement to provide a tangible way to demonstrate commitment by both parties. The paid mentor has a responsibility and accountability to help the mentee to achieve their goals, overcome the challenges that will arise, and develop the skills necessary for success in their role. As women, we often give of ourselves and our time as volunteers. It becomes essential for our own well-being that we are consistently reminded of our worth. If the mentor/mentee relationship is a compensated commitment, let us proceed unapologetically.

## TIME IS VALUABLE

Women in the organization who are aspiring and perceive an experienced mentor to be a catalyst for achieving their next step or women who appreciate guidance in their current role, but do not have access to outside funding or district level support, will generally seek a mentor on their own in a much more informal relationship.

Some districts offer formally mentoring programs that are sanctioned and supported by the organization. Some offer stipends, while others rely on the intrinsic motivation of paying it forward. How the mentors are chosen becomes a significant factor of the benefit of programs where the organization is at the helm. Studies have shown that few formal in-house mentoring programs are effective or meeting their intended goals. This is due to the pairing that is often random and based on limited commonality (Davila & Gotian, 2023).

### Are We Compatible?

*Jody has just been appointed as a new superintendent and was delighted to negotiate a paid mentor for Year 1 of her contract. Jody knew of a retired superintendent in the county with an outstanding reputation and contacted her to inquire if she had the time and space to serve as her mentor. Teresa, the experienced, retired superintendent, was flattered and interested but was concerned that Jody may not find her style, communication skills, or demeanor to be compatible, so she insisted they have an informal lunch together before this decision was finalized. They met for lunch twice, and at the end of the second lunch, the mentee confirmed that she was comfortable, confident, and excited to ask Teresa again to be her mentor. Teresa enthusiastically agreed, and they joined into a formal mentoring contract. They continued to meet for lunch on a regular basis, and their meetings were focused, regular, and productive.*

To pay or not to pay depends on what you need as the mentee. If you do not pay the mentor, you may not get what you need, but you do receive the gift of time and expertise of a colleague. On the other hand, if the mentor is paid, there is structure to the relationship. Meetings are regulated and occur at agreed times and places. The mentor is aware of your goals, your specific needs, and works to ensure that you have access and opportunity through those agreements.

The end goal, regardless of the compensation factor, is to create a sustainable and effective mentor/mentee relationship.

## BLENDING AND PRIORITIES

To find the time for a mentoring relationship, it is necessary to delve into the barriers of personal and professional blending as we examine balance as a process and not an event. Balance is not the destination, it is the constant state of revision, adjustment, and fine-tuning. This ongoing effort requires continuous modifications of our blending of priorities and a deep dive into what truly matters in our personal and professional journey. We can learn to decline opportunities and invitations that do not align with our goals to ultimately create space for what is truly important and what genuinely matters to us. Thus, we strive to blend our professional lives and our personal lives, with less emphasis on the ultimate event of "finding or creating balance." If we find our priorities slipping out of alignment, we must seize the opportunity to reassess. What is causing the imbalance?

Are there practices we can employ to ground ourselves and open space for what truly matters? Is the concept that relationships precede learning in line with our everyday activities that consume time and space? Often, we find that our own well-being is first to be postponed when we are out of balance. We quickly discontinue attention of activities that promote our physical and mental health. Are we prioritizing fitness, sleep, and nutrition for our loved ones but not necessarily for ourselves? Is it any wonder that we run out of steam and begin to feel like we are failing in our personal and professional lives?

Balance is not something we obtain if we just try harder, especially when we are in constant motion. Author and culture design consultant, Gustavo Razzetti (2018) recognized that balance is a noun and a verb. Thus, balance is less about how we divide our time and more about what we are doing at any moment in time. He suggested that we integrate our professional and personal lives and discontinue the departmentalizing of work and personal life.

Trudy recalls inviting her husband for Friday night "dates" to include music, sports, and food. When he enthusiastically accepted, she then let him know that their date would begin in the high school auditorium with the wind ensemble, followed by the second half of the varsity football game, and nourished by tailgate hotdogs with the Booster Club! She knew she was pushing it, but they managed to have fun and be together, and Trudy was able to attend the functions required as the superintendent. They found a balanced combination of what they wanted to do and, in this case, what she needed to do. Finding the time to be in a mentoring relationship may require reallocating the time you have and seeking new ways to create time.

## ARE YOU A PERFECTIONIST?

We all feel out of balance periodically. It is usually cyclical. If we follow an academic calendar, perhaps we find ourselves out of balance at the beginning of a school year, during the holidays, and at the end of the school year. These seasons in our lives require adjustment and grace for ourselves. External factors such as politics, racism, gender roles, sexism, and economic hardships foster additional burdens for many to endure. Cultural norms can also add to the stress of creating that balance. As we see those months approaching, it may require a "best as I can" attitude, versus the perfectionist mentality. The focus is not about getting through the month; it is about moving through the month to the best of our abilities with joy and satisfaction for the effort that we put into the equation. Do the holiday cookies have to be homemade? Does the schedule have to be laminated? Do your own children have to participate in crazy hair day? Do you have to be at every holiday event, or can you designate others to share the opportunities?

## DO OUR ACTIONS SUPPORT OUR VALUES?

It is time to seek out other women for support and to share our stories and strategies. It is time to lift each other up when we are struggling and dance with each other when we are thriving. It is time to go back to your "why" and make certain that your actions indeed reflect your values. There have been so many times in our lives, particularly as young women, when we were challenged to check on our alignment with our values and actions. Do you recall a time when your partner said that they were tired of being the bottom rung of your ladder? Or the time when a parent or a dear friend expressed sadness that they never see you even though they live in the same town? If those are familiar examples, perhaps it is time to reassess. *Time* is the key word.

What examples do you have of times in your personal life that your actions have not aligned with your values?

___________________________________________________________

___________________________________________________________

___________________________________________________________

___________________________________________________________

### Barriers: Systems of Oppression and Entitlement

As we examine the barrier of time, it is important to note that The Tools of Cultural Proficiency provide us with a framework to identify the barriers to becoming a mentor or a mentee. Although women have prepared themselves well to be educational leaders, barriers continue to exist in the forms of oppression and entitlement. We were informed by a district that a *Leading While Female* after school book club was questioned and ultimately prohibited as it was deemed to be exclusive. Women were not allowed to foster the relationships of mentors and sponsors in this previously organized environment. The women attempted to find the time to form an affinity group to develop mentoring relationships, but systems of oppression prohibited this from becoming their reality.

The barriers that were previously identified, such as traditional pathways, traditional roles, and hiring practices, continue to be prevalent. Without mentors to guide us, we are more likely to be static. A female in a neighboring county was interviewing for a superintendent position and was advised by a male search firm consultant not to bring her purse to the next step in the interview process. He stated that it was too messy, and the purse served as a reminder to the panel that she was a woman. She took the advice reluctantly and did not bring a purse to the final interview. As she was leaving the final interview, a male trustee on the interview panel asked her if she had everything! She expressed her dismay to not have had a female mentor to share her story and assist her with a decision as mundane as a purse . . . but so relevant in the interview process of the job she was trying to secure.

We have all been to educational conferences, and at the end of the day, the scenario generally looks the same. Our male allies and colleagues gather in the lobby, at the bar or even on the golf course. Generally, females go straight to the room and check emails, inquire about home activities, check on family dinner plans, homework, baths, and bedtime. Traditional roles do not always foster the opportunity to converse with mentors and mentees. How might we alter the narrative and create that time for mentoring? Might a women in leadership daily afternoon or morning session be provided within the timeframe of the conference? Might the female leaders with 10+ years of experience host a gathering for all the new female leaders? Perhaps our male allies could encourage us to join in as they introduce us to others in an informal network. Might there be a dinner just for women after they have checked in on their home situations? Women who have traditional roles in their homes are unapologetic in their decisions. The woman does not need to change, but the system can be altered to increase networking and mentoring opportunities for female leaders. If "that's the way it's always been" is our response, it is time for a follow-up question. Is that the way it should always be?

## Protecting Time in the Mentoring Relationship

Time efficiency will be a critical component in the mentoring relationship. Because time is both a valuable asset and often a barrier, it becomes necessary to ensure time effectiveness in the relationship itself. As a mentor, ensure that your mentoring sessions are well planned and efficient without being rushed or overly scheduled. Verify with your mentee what they might want to discuss in the upcoming meeting in advance so that you can be prepared with thoughts, ideas, and resources. At the onset of the meeting, begin with accomplishments, sources of pride, and successes. Be prepared to follow up with what was discussed in the previous session to ensure closure or necessary extension. To be sure that time is well spent in the session, leave space for emotion and vulnerability as well as content and guidance. As you conclude the meeting, clarify next steps as well as the next meeting time and place. Place it on your calendar to ensure that commitments are valued and time is sacred. Follow after the meeting with texts, phone calls, and resources, and be sure that your mentee is clear that you are available without appointments as needs arise.

Carving out time to be in a mentoring relationship will require an audit of the time you currently spend on others. We are challenged to find ways to alternate that schedule so there is time to spend on our own personal and professional growth. If time is identified as the female leader's greatest barrier to entering a mentoring relationship, and lack of female mentoring has been identified as a significant barrier to securing leadership positions, then we must figure out how to balance and prioritize the time to move forward. The following are some everyday leadership suggestions to assist you in freeing up time so that you, too, can be in a mentoring relationship:

- Make sure that your calendar includes tasks that you need to do for yourself, not just tasks that need to be done for others. If you have a letter of recommendation to write or a board letter to prepare, make sure it is on your calendar and not something that will be done on Sunday afternoon at your own expense.

- Train your administrative assistant to interrupt meetings at the designated times for the meeting to conclude. A 1-hour meeting that turns into a 2-hour meeting takes away from your time.

- Model beginning and ending times of meetings when you are conducting a meeting, knowing that the woman is the one that traditionally has personal obligations at the conclusion of the professional workday.

- Delegate and use the skills and job expectations of others. Often, we think we must do it all. We are disrespecting those who have the skills and the job description to do some of the work that we have taken on.

- Walk and talk during one-on-one meetings. Find ways to combine work with personal goals so that the walk does not have to be an additional hour in the day.

- Be reminded that "no" is an option and a complete sentence.

- Work with your assistants to open your mail, reroute your emails, and maintain your calendar.

- Prioritize your tasks and chunk them so that the work can get done in small parts, if necessary.

- Organize your files, workspace, and daily actions so that all is within reach and at your fingertips.

- Take breaks so that you are not exhausted by the day's end. Sit down, and eat, breathe, rest your eyes, or meditate during the workday.

- Create empty calendar days. It is incredible how much you can get done when there is nothing on your calendar.

- Integrate artificial intelligence (AI) into your daily practice to streamline and enhance operations and administration.

What might be some time-savers that you have discovered to allow you to create time for a mentoring relationship? Share your time-savers with your female colleagues.

_______________________________________________

_______________________________________________

_______________________________________________

_______________________________________________

Chapter 5 identifies the roles and responsibilities of the mentor as well as the purpose and importance of a mentoring program. Dive in to create the best possible mentoring relationship for you and your partner.

# CHAPTER 5

# WHAT'S MY ROLE?

## Roles, Responsibilities, and Relationships

*The richness of differences and diversity make us as individuals and as organizations even stronger. And therein lies the purpose of mentoring.*

Arriaga et al. (in press)

Mentor programs are designed to support career growth and development. Traditionally, the three well-known types of mentoring have been formal, informal, and peer-to-peer. Various virtual meeting technology options are available for mentors supporting career planning. That said, technology hasn't changed the fact that successful mentee/mentor relationships are collaborative, learning-centered, purposeful, competency-driven, and career-focused. These characteristics are at the core of both in-person and virtual mentoring relationships. This chapter presents the purposes and importance of mentoring programs. Additionally, the roles and responsibilities of mentee and mentor are delineated.

One of the critical aspects of the mentoring relationship is for the mentee and mentor to clarify their roles and responsibilities. Irrespective of which corporate or educational executive leadership roles they hold, mentors and role models are part of leadership development, formal and informal. In 1985, Dr. Kathy Kram of Boston University, Graduate School of Business described the mentoring relationship as being developmental and beneficial to both mentee and mentor. Prior to Kram's developmental description of both participants moving through beneficial phases, research had focused mainly on the benefit of the relationship to the protégé/mentee rather than the mentor. Over the years, however, the definition of mentor clearly holds the most responsibility, as in the Cambridge Online Dictionary definition (https://dictionary.cambridge.org/dictionary/english/mentor?q=Mentor): *mentor is a person who gives an often younger or less experienced person help and advice over a period of time, especially at work or school.* Kram's foundational work identified the role of mentor to be helping her protege by providing two general types of behaviors or functions:

- Career development functions, which facilitate the protege's advancement in the organization
- Psychosocial functions, which contribute to the protege's personal growth and professional development (Kram, 1985)

These two mentor functions hold true even today. Kram's study of protégé-mentor relationship revealed four developmental phases:

- **Initiation phase**—introduction, early stage of relationship (get acquainted strategies)
- **Cultivation phase**—range of functions expand to maximum of relationship/friendship career supporting exchanges, long term confirmation of trust (friends, sponsorships, recommendations)
- **Separation phase**—organizational structures change the nature of the relationship and may alter psychological needs of one or both individuals (protégé gets new job)
- **Redefinition phase**—relationship evolves into a different form than the past (relationship develops into being peers or ends completely)

A mentor's relationship certainly has the potential to impact and enhance the career development of both mentee and mentor. Kram's relationship study (1985) illustrated how both individuals benefited. The young manager and the senior manager are provided opportunities for growth in two areas of career and psychological functions.

The reciprocity of the mentee/mentor relationship is illustrated when one career function of the mentor is to guide the mentee through networking opportunities, each individual benefits in different ways. For example, while the mentee experiences the importance of belonging to a regional sister circle, the mentor benefits from opportunities to get acquainted with executive leaders from other schools and districts and may connect with members of the higher education community in support of her own career path. The mentee and mentor both benefit from the networking experience.

## ROLES OF MENTEES AND MENTORS

A mentor is often identified as the traditional all-encompassing coach, guide, and role model. In addition to the traditional mentor, sponsors may join the support team for leaders. Sponsors are senior people in the organization with the power to promote and to create visibility for emerging, talented leaders. Some organizations include executive coaches hired to provide certain kinds of supportive functions. These various mentor roles may comprise a network that an individual enlists into their own career development plan. Monica Higgins and Kathy Kram (2001) identified "developmental networks" in the early 2000s because they observed women seeking only one mentor was a limiting factor for their career planning. More than likely, since most organizations had male-dominated executive leaders as in the education field, one mentor would be male. The absence of female role models as executive leadership for many years made it almost impossible for women to have a sense of self as a leader. Having a sense of oneself as a leader is one of the basic reasons Higgins and Kram (2001) expanded the idea of mentoring to include the developmental network, a set of relationships that support the female leader with aspirations for career advancement.

## ROLE OF THE MENTEE

The mentee is responsible for taking the initiative and seeking a mentor. The mentee identifies her own needs and desired/expected outcomes of the relationship. Mentees maintain confidentiality, assist in goal setting, identify objectives for learning, and anticipate challenges. Following these guidelines enhances the mentoring relationship and supports effective personal growth. The mentee takes the lead in the relationship and primarily establishes her learning objectives, keeps on task, honors the timeline established by the mentor, and evaluates the quality of the relationship. As with any relationship, both parties have responsibilities. Some of the responsibilities include, but are not limited to those listed in Table 5.1:

**Table 5.1** · *Responsibilities of Mentees and Mentors*

| Mentee | Mentor |
| --- | --- |
| • Take initiative in the relationship and establish short- and long-term career goals | • Serve as a positive role model |
| • Keep commitments with the mentor | • Help identify skill gaps and challenge the mentee |

*(Continued)*

(Continued)

| Mentee | Mentor |
|---|---|
| • Maintain confidentiality, always | • Listen well |
| • Be open to receiving feedback and coaching | • Provide safe risk-taking environment and encourage mentee to explore new ideas |
| • Take responsibility for professional growth and development | • Celebrate mentee milestones and achievements |
| • Seek challenging assignments | • Serve as a source of information and resources |
| • Reflect on progress and future planning | • Ask mediational questions, facilitate mentee's thinking |
| • Renegotiate the mentoring relationship as needs change | • Hold mentee accountable |
| • Show gratitude for the mentor's time and expertise | • Be aware of signals indicating it may be time to end the relationship |
| • Bring relationship to a close | • Follow lead of mentee to close relationship |

Adapted from University of Texas at Austin Human Resources (https://hr.utexas.edu/manager/tools/mentoring webpage)

Table 5.1 indicates the importance of the mentee to take the lead in the relationship and establish career goals. Once the mentee has achieved her goals, the mentee and mentor decide how to close or continue the mentoring relationship.

## Reflections

As you review the roles and responsibilities of mentee and mentors, what challenges might each face?

___________________________________________________________

___________________________________________________________

What benefits have you experienced as a mentee?

_______________________________________________

_______________________________________________

What benefits have you experienced as a mentor?

_______________________________________________

_______________________________________________

## HUMAN RESOURCES/PERSONNEL DEPARTMENTS

### Building a Developmental Network

The vital function of a school district's human resource department is, of course, managing all aspects of employment and staff development. These functions include, but are not limited to, recruitment, employee relations, performance management, legal compliance, and professional development. The success of a district may be determined by how willing the local board is to invest in the development of its people.

District and site budgets are built on time, people, and materials. Both time and materials are only as good as the people employed who use them. Therefore, investing in growing people makes sense. Looking at this investment in people as educational, or professional, capital, Hargreaves and Fullan (2013) describe professional capital as a necessary investment in people within the school district. In other words, the district is willing to use capital to invest in teacher growth, leadership development, and career paths. Professional capital is comprised of the following:

- Human capital—the talent of individuals acquired through equitable hiring practices

- Social capital—the collaborative power of the group established and transferred as organizational cultural

- Decisional capital—sound, expert, wise judgments made about learners who are cultivated over many years (Hargreaves & Fullan, 2013)

Clearly, one way to invest in *growing our own* teacher leaders and the next generation of administrators is through a mentoring program. For example, human resources departments recruit and attract leaders who have stellar referrals from regional mentoring networks. Once hired, leaders are supported by senior executive leaders to learn the *district way*. As Hargreaves & Fullan (2013) explained, human capital is built through equitable hiring practices to ensure the district has the most qualified and diverse workforce to best serve its community. Social capital, typically viewed as a set of shared values or resources that allow individuals to work together toward a common purpose, is developed to sustain the employment of the best hired. And professional capital is developed through a set of learned behaviors to support the organizational culture of *the way we do business around here*. Mentor programs are designed to support districtwide investment in *our way* through executive leadership. For example, the district investment in a mentor program is an investment in people:

- **Step 1—Hire the Best** (Human Capital)
  - Employ equitable hiring practices.
  - Support employees after hiring: mentor program focused on "the district way," for new employees to learn organizational culture.

- **Step 2—Develop Supportive Networks** (Social Capital)
  - Grow reciprocal relationships for mentee and mentor.
  - Develop networks for *the district way*.

- **Step 3—Develop Peer Pods** (Professional Capital)
  - Use professional learning strategies to train mentee/mentor pair as peers so that the mentee becomes a mentor to grow *the district way* and support emerging and executive female leaders throughout the district.

- **Step 4—Monitor and Adjust** (Professional Capital)
  - Establish benchmarks for program and mentee/mentor successes.
  - Monitor, measure, and publish successes.
  - Establish a continuous improvement cycle, beginning with equitable recruiting and hiring practices.

The Professional Capital Model clearly invests in growing leaders with shared values and vision for the district. A mentor program is designed to support executive leaders within the organization. The overarching purpose of the program is to identify highly qualified women leaders and support them as they are *Leading While Female*.

**Vignette**

*Sometimes It Takes Ten!*

*It came to Juana's attention that her male middle school principal was not supporting a letter of recommendation because the Title 1 position that she currently held was written around her talents and skills. She was too valuable in her current position to lose to a promotion. Juana responded by asking ten women to write letters of recommendation on her behalf. This mentoring, sponsorship, and support resulted in securing her first district-level position. Her new female superintendent informed her that she attempted to contact the male middle school principal, but he never returned the call. She based her decision to hire on all the letters and the calls with women who wrote the letters. The superintendent has become her mentor, sponsor, and coach in her new role and has helped her to navigate the politics in a psychologically safe environment.*

## ADDITIONAL CAPITAL GAINS

Research shows women leaders have expressed no less desire than do men for promotions to leadership roles. However, this ambition is met with far greater barriers to success for women than for men. In their recent ground-breaking research about women overcoming those barriers, Ellingrud et al. (2025) introduced the concept of *experience capital*. The authors explained that across the average career trajectory, half a person's earnings come from what they know and what they can do. The second half of their earnings come from the value of their skills and experiences gained on the job. Additionally, their research showed women were not accumulating experience capital at the same rates as their male counter parts. This slower rate of building experience capital is not the fault of women, nor is it the task of women to fix the problem. Structural, or systems barriers, such as recent and current policies, practices, programs, and procedures have existed that systematically hold women back in the workplace.

An example of a lack of *experience capital* in the educational field is the rapid promotions of men from teacher to principal and onto superintendent while their female counterpart awaits having access to matched leadership skills to those of football coach, athletic director, or assistant principal for discipline. In our earlier work (Arriaga et al., 2020), we found female educators tend to wait until they have met all requirements for a leadership position, while the male educator may apply when he reaches about 75 percent to 80 percent qualified for the leadership position. While the HR department is providing opportunities for professional capital for candidates, each female candidate has the responsibility to develop and publish her *experience capital*.

## REVERSE MENTORING DRIVES DIVERSITY AND IMPROVES LEADERSHIP

A growing interest is occurring in flipping the traditional mentee/mentor model. Rather than the mentor being the more experienced of the two, the mentee is less experienced by title, yet more experienced by background and life experience and professional training. For example, Teresa, a Latina and director of technology and instruction, has had Carina, assistant superintendent for instruction, also Latina, as her mentor for 2 years. Teresa aspires to be superintendent within the next 5 years, and Carina is supporting her toward achieving that goal. In the meantime, Linda, the first African American female superintendent for the district has asked Teresa to be her mentor for the use of technology, specifically artificial intelligence and data analysis. Linda's technology skills are limited, and her goal is to develop understanding and use of new platforms for displaying districtwide data through district available communication tools.

Flipping the traditional model of age and experience driving the mentor program, reverse mentoring highlights identity, hierarchy, culture change, diversity, inclusion, and compassion for aspiring as well as experienced leaders (O'Connor et al., 2024). The examples of Teresa, Carina, and Linda illustrate transformational opportunities for cross-generational and cross-cultural conversations.

## ORGANIZATIONS BENEFIT FROM LEADING WHILE FEMALE MENTOR PROGRAM

School districts and organizations benefit from mentor programs with clearly stated purposes and well-designed outcomes. Due to the complex nature of the job and the rapid turnover rate of the job of superintendent, 38 percent of large districts in the United States changed leaders between September 2020 and September 2022 (Superville, 2022). Because of the changes in the leadership role, some state and national organizations have developed mentoring programs for superintendents. These programs are designed to refine and formalize developmental networks and relationships that can help new superintendents grow in their roles as leaders. Irrespective of how the programs are designed, one aspect holds true. The relationship between mentee and mentor is reciprocal. Both individuals benefit from sharing emerging issues and charting paths for strategies that may apply in both careers.

The purposes of a well-designed mentor program include, but are not limited to,

- facilitating growth and development of high-potential leaders,

- demonstrating visible commitment to professional development and continuous learning,

- transferring and maintaining institutional knowledge, and

- fostering an inclusive, diverse, and collaborative environment.

With these purposes in mind, organizations and school districts can establish mentor programs to benefit the mentee and mentors as well as the organization itself. Human resources departments can establish high-quality mentor programs using The Professional Capital Model:

- **Step 1**—Select a talent team. Find people who want to serve as leadership team members to develop a mentor program

- **Step 2**—The talent team determines high-level, measurable goals. Write at least three SMART goals.

- **Step 3**—Invite employees to register for participation.

- **Step 4**—Make matches. The talent team determines the process for matching mentees and mentors.

- **Step 5**—Provide professional learning for mentors to foster an inclusive, diverse, and collaborative environment and to transfer and maintain institutional knowledge.

- **Step 6**—Measure mentor program success and publish success toward goals.

Honest inclusivity means more than addressing compliance accommodations or checklist items. Inclusivity is both *vision* and *practice* for the way organizations function (Lindsey et al., 2018). McKinsey & Company is an international, values-driven organization that helps clients pursue sustainability, inclusion, and growth. They partner with their clients *to innovate more sustainably, achieve lasting gains in performance, and build workforces that will thrive for this generation and the next* (McKinsey & Company, 2024). The workplace is intentionally designed as a welcoming, accessible, supportive environment where all employees can thrive irrespective of their unique needs. Diverse languages, talents, ethnicities, cultures, and abilities are viewed as assets rather than liabilities. True diversity and inclusion are embraced and celebrated to proactively address organizational barriers. Intentionally designing mentor programs to transfer a culture of inclusion and belonging ensures a workplace that is continuously welcoming and accessible and fosters a culture where everyone can thrive. Following are questions their talent attraction teams (human resources) keep in mind:

1. Are we leading or lagging in accessibility? When we look at the world around us, does it feel like we've done everything we could?

2. Do we have a clearly defined ambition for accessibility? What does success look like for our organization?

3. Are we investing in the right areas to create the greatest impact? Are our resources aligned with the needs of our colleagues?

While these questions are not new to human resources and diversity and inclusion teams, it's important to regularly revisit them to ensure the school system is on track.

Investing in areas of greatest impact is a combination of human capital, social capital, and professional capital. Well-planned and closely monitored mentor programs and networks are beneficial to emerging leaders, veteran leaders, and the organization itself. However, if close examination of hiring policies and practices using the lens of Cultural Proficiency reveals the organizational status quo doesn't serve growth opportunities for women leaders, especially women of color, then maybe it's time to invest (human capital) in historically marginalized groups, especially women of color. Data from our inquiry and other studies reveal the current context of *leading while female*.

## WOMEN-TO-WOMEN IS IMPORTANT

Although women executive leaders are making gains in the workplace, progress is not enough, nor fast enough. The struggle remains for some women to gain access to the organizations' higher decision-making levels. Mentoring programs are designed for more women to advance to the executive leadership roles for access to the power structure. Mentoring consultant company Mentoring Complete (2025) identified women's difficulties in finding mentors and reasons to offer mentor programs:

- Successful and highly powerful women may resist mentoring another woman for fear of creating a future competitor within the company.

- Since specific laws govern appropriate behavior in the workplace, men may be reluctant to initiate mentoring a woman for fear of negative repercussions.

Nevertheless, women need professional mentoring experiences to give them access to upper levels of school districts and organizations. Irrespective of challenges, organizations should offer women-to women-mentoring. Here are four very compelling reasons why:

- **Cross-cultural mentoring programs make a strong case for diversity inclusion initiatives.** Today's workforce is evolving to become increasingly diverse. Successful organizations are fostering diversity initiatives to provide collaboration across different demographic groups. However, some diversity initiatives fall short of their goals for overcoming institutional barriers. Mentoring programs can serve as a highly effective technique to reduce the barriers to equal access. Some organizations offer mentor programs within the context of their overall performance goals that help achieve diversity and equity goals.

- **A good mentor focuses on the mentee's total development**. A mentor guides the mentee using specific skills, sharing resources and network contacts, challenging the mentee to take risks, all within the context of a safe learning environment.

- **The mentor transfers self-confidence, communication skills, and realistic self-assessment for the mentee.** In a cross-cultural woman-to-woman mentoring relationship, the mentor and mentee will both benefit from the relationship.

- **The true benefit and impact of mentoring is in the personal exchange between the mentor and mentee.** Successful mentoring creates true relationships. These relationships are especially beneficial for organizations committed to promoting diversity.

- **Mentoring remains an important equitable hiring tool for organizations to recruit and retain a diverse workforce**. Women-to-women mentoring fosters relationships while developing and retaining talent throughout the organization.

### Reflections

**As you think about the previous section, what might be some reasons mentoring programs are important to female leaders?**

_______________________________________________

_______________________________________________


**As you think about the previous section, what might be some reasons mentoring programs are important to school districts?**

_______________________________________________

_______________________________________________

As districts and organizations design human resources programs in support of women advancing along their career paths, barriers (professional and personal) continue to get in their way. Our inquiry revealed data worth a closer examination.

## DATA REVEALED THROUGH STORIES
### Professional Barriers

Barriers keeping women leaders from advancing along their career paths at the same rate as their male counterparts have been intentionally structured within organizations to maintain the status quo. Since 91.3 percent of chief executive officers, chief financial officers, and chief operations officers are male (McKinsey & Company, 2024), they continue to fill their roles with candidates who look just like them and behave in similar ways. This majority White, male workforce will continue to be the dominate narrative unless these same White male leaders intentionally seek to change the culture of organizations to that of more diverse, equitable, and inclusive workplaces. Data from our inquiry revealed the following barriers from the participants:

>**Organizational Culture.** The culture within an organization can either support or hinder career paths for female leaders. In environments where gender biases and stereotypes are prevalent, female leaders may struggle to gain respect and opportunities they deserve, impacting their ability to advance in the organization and mentor others effectively.

**Access to Opportunities.** Limited access to professional leadership roles, networking groups, and sponsorships can be barriers for female leaders. Without these opportunities, female leaders can be slow to advance in their careers and serve as effective mentors.

**Organizational Support Systems.** A strong professional support system is crucial for female leaders. A lack of an intentional organizational leadership structure can make managing their responsibilities and pursuing career growth extremely difficult for emerging female leaders. Built-in supports include, but are not limited to, formal mentoring programs in which high level male leaders mentor executive female leaders.

> *Women face distinct barriers that programs to develop and advance women can help address. Yet there's been a decline in career development, mentorship, and sponsorship programs geared toward women—and relatively few companies track the outcomes of these programs. In addition, there has been a sharp decline in recruiting and internship programs focused on women. And in all cases, companies are investing in fewer programs designed to advance women of color.*
>
> McKinsey & Company (2024) p.16

## PERSONAL BARRIERS

Not only do organizational culture and structure serve as barriers to females advancing their careers, often, we seem to get in our own way. Many women have more difficulty finding balance between home and career advancement than our male counterparts. Female leaders may delay their advancement waiting to develop more confidence and competence before moving to the next level.

Overcoming personal barriers is one of the benefits of working with a mentor. As indicated by our inquiry participants, often leaders do not see the barriers until the mentor calls them out. Personal barriers to career advancement described by inquiry participants included the following categories:

- **Work-Life Imbalance.** Many female leaders face the challenge of balancing professional responsibilities with personal and family commitments. These challenges might lead to feelings of being overwhelmed, depressed, and stressed. Without a work-life balance, female leaders find difficulty focusing on career advancement and mentorship.

- **Lack of Self-Confidence.** A significant barrier for both mentors and mentees can be a lack of self-confidence. Female leaders may doubt their abilities or feel unqualified for leadership roles. These feelings of "not good enough" might hinder their professional growth and their effectiveness as leaders and mentors. An inquiry participant stated,

> I mentor women leaders with doctoral degrees at the top of the education field. The thread that has been consistent through most every conversation is their lack of belief in themselves. They constantly wonder if they are prepared enough, if they have the "it" factor, if they are "well rounded" enough. My work is to help build their confidence so they will take that next step and reach beyond what their current belief system is telling them they can do.
>
> Current Superintendent Mentor, White, Female

- **Individual preferences and biases.** Preference factors include personal biases of individuals who hold the fate of a leader in their hands. One of our inquiry participants described an unfortunate situation that illustrated personal bias:

> I witnessed a highly qualified candidate be thwarted in an interview process by a board member who took exception to "her roots were showing, and her manicure wasn't fresh." Little did the interview team know the candidate had taken a red eye flight for the interview after taking care of her mom following the funeral of a close relative. The district lost a great candidate.
>
> Retired Superintendent Mentor, White, Female

Preference factors also arise based on immutable characteristics a leader may have that are not discussed openly but are shared privately. These characteristics include, but are not limited to, body shape, speech pattern, voice volume (too loud or soft spoken), clothing styles, make-up (too much or not enough), and hair style/color. For example, one candidate was told privately that African American females who wore natural hair styles should not apply in their district. In another district, a female leader was told she always interrupts and talks too loudly, and supervisors frown on that behavior in the district. These characteristics sometimes become topics between mentor and mentee. The question from the mentee to the mentor may be, *to what degree am I willing to give up part of who I am to become who they want me to be* (fit the mold)? Or the question from the mentor to the mentee might be, *to what degree are you willing to consider changing part of who you are to match their expectations?*

The need for women mentoring women is to help women advance in their careers and to develop their leadership skills. Women mentoring women can also help create a more equitable workplace. Clearly, when organizations develop mentoring programs for women, the women grow in the following ways:

- **Builds confidence**: Women mentoring women can help build self-confidence and communication skills.

- **Improves self-assessment**: Women mentoring women can help women develop a realistic sense of self-assessment.

- **Increases leadership opportunities**: Women mentoring women can help more women enter leadership roles.

When women grow and advance in the organization, clearly the organization grows and benefits. Mentors improve their skills by keeping these behaviors in mind:

- **Be a good listener**: Actively listen to your mentee and give them honest feedback.

- **Be dependable**: Mentees need consistency from their mentor.

- **Be a friend**: Focus on having fun and validating your mentee's feelings and goals.

- **Be available**: Make time for your mentee and invest in her success.

## MENTORING REALLY MATTERS

This chapter provided roles, responsibilities of mentors, and the importance of developing mentor programs. The goal of Leading While Female mentoring is to recognize the importance of women mentoring women along their career paths. Although we emphasize women-to-women relationships, we are not suggesting we are all alike. We learn much more from those who are different from ourselves. The richness of differences and diversity makes us as individuals and as organizations even stronger. And therein lies the purpose of mentoring.

## Reflections

As you reflect on the content of this chapter, what might be key ideas that inform your career planning?

_______________________________________________

_______________________________________________

In what ways might you continue to build your developmental network?

_______________________________________________

_______________________________________________

Chapter 6 is a reminder that career development is all about the mentee and mentor relationship. The use of breakthrough questions is essential to fostering relationships and moving to the next steps for advancement.

# BREAKING THROUGH THE MOMENTUM

*To be conscious is to be aware of one's thoughts, feelings, viewpoints, and behavior and the effect they have on others. Consciousness serves as the coaches' resource for being attentive to the verbal, non-verbal, and cultural cues of the person being coached.*

– Robert Garmston and Delores Lindsey

As you've learned from previous chapters, mentoring is specific to having either senior, midlevel, and even peers show mentees the ropes, specifically for a position of interest, and offer support through the complex and sometimes perplexing journey toward ultimate career goals (Alpaio, 2024). The goal of this chapter is to expand the information from Chapter 1 and the role coaching plays in the mentoring process. Whether for the mentee or mentor, coaching is a tool and skillset used to support the relationship for growth and progress toward goals. By the end of this chapter, mentees will learn what to ask for, and mentors will learn best practices for asking breakthrough questions designed for female leaders.

The idea of coaching has been around for centuries and may be traced back to the Socratic era when "philosophers used questioning and dialogue to help individuals clarify their thinking and achieve their goals" (ThomasFisk, 2024). As time continued, the concept of coaching was used in the context of sports (circa 1880s); then in the early 20th century coaching surfaced in the education field as a way to foster student educational success. By the mid-20th century and to the present day, coaching became valued across industries to support the professional development of its employees (The History of Coaching, 2024). The 21st century brought these dynamic development models into the education field; intentionally allowing teachers to be coached in ways for them to delve into their metacognitive thought processes and bring to consciousness the "why" around their instructional practice. Experts, including Robert Dilts (1994), Arthur Costa and Robert Garmston (1994), provided conceptual frameworks as tools for supporting the coach. Researchers Lindsey et al. (2007) extended this foundation to encompass a framework that seeks to engage the dignity of the coachee/mentee as the foundation for the mentoring through coaching relationship. Table 6.0, from the seminal *Culturally Proficient Coaching* text, displays the intersection of coaching, states of mind, and Cultural Proficiency.

## IT'S ALL ABOUT RELATIONSHIPS!

The mentor uses coaching skills to guide the conversation toward growth. Notice in Table 6.0, the intersections of The Tools of Cultural Proficiency and cognitive coaching (states of mind) models rest on rapport, trust, and effective communication. Authentic relationships are a key tenet of thoughtful, respectful, and mutually beneficial mentoring partnerships. The authenticity of coaching leads the mentor to listen with intent to understand the mentee's grounding. Likewise, the mentor creates an authentic environment where the mentee feels safe enough to be transparent and vulnerable. This safe environment allows both the mentee and mentor to share significant and personal information.

**Table 6.0** • *Cultural Proficiency Alignment Cognitive Coaching (Lindsey et al., 2007)*

| | |
|---|---|
| **Five Essential Elements** serve as standards for measuring mentee growth toward culturally proficient values, behaviors, policies, and practice. | **Five States of Mind** are internal resources that mentors and mentees harness to inform human perception. |
| **Guiding Principles** serve as core values for mentors and mentees. | **Propositions of Cognitive Coaching** used by mentors clarify behavioral changes based on changes in thinking. |
| **Cultural Proficiency Continuum** provides for a shift from unhealthy and nonproductive policies, practices, and behaviors to healthy, positive, productive behaviors and policies that allow the mentor to focus on the needs of their female mentees. | **Cognitive Coaching Capabilities and Skills** assume intentions and choices to support the mentee in shifts of thinking and changes of behaviors. |

| | |
|---|---|
| **Cultural Proficiency** is an individual's values, beliefs, and assumptions and the organization's policies and practices. It is critical for mentors as they seek to support women leaders in their growth and career advancement. | **Cognitive Coaching Addresses** individual capabilities and supports group development. |
| **Cultural Proficiency** is a nonjudgmental, nonevaluative conversation. | **Cognitive Coaching** is a nonjudgmental, nonevaluative conversation. |
| **Culturally Proficient Interactions** are based on rapport, trust, and effective communication skills. | **Cognitive Coaching Interactions** are based on rapport, trust, and effective communication skills. |

Table 6.1 is the Cultural Proficiency map in the mentor's head for guiding the goal-focused conversation. The social-political landscape of today's schools and communities requires leaders to be *in their heads* throughout their working day and often well beyond. The expectation for schools to support the psychological and physical safety of students and staff elevates the need for school district leaders to be thoughtful in their decision-making in a consistent and coherent manner. Moreover, just when a leader believes they've successfully de-escalated their community about various high-tension matters, another important matter rears its head. Female mentors can hold the five states of mind as their internal resources and, at the same time, navigate critical matters using The Tools of Cultural Proficiency.

Compounding and critical factors facing schools and corporate organizations have led to the frequent turnover of c-suite leaders in education, and recent research shows that districts are struggling with the retention of superintendents. In a December 2024 AASA survey, 24.5 percent of superintendents identified as serving 10 years or more in the same district assignment, down from 41.5% in 2000 (AASA, 2024). With this concerning statistic in mind, educational leaders must have continuous, high-quality culturally proficient mentoring conversations that pose reflective questions with the intent of fostering quality day-to-day leadership moves and decision making.

## QUALITY RELATIONSHIPS YIELD QUALITY MENTORING: WHY CONTEXT MATTERS

When the intersectionality of gender, race, or ethnicity is added to the critical environment, mentors must focus on using the attributes of culturally proficient coaching as a light to illuminate the complexities. Let's walk through this example:

Background

> *Yanil is in her third year serving as the superintendent of a district that has grown in the number of students of color—mostly of the Asian diaspora who identify as Karen from Burma. Yanil herself is a first-generation immigrant and holds compassionate understanding for the challenges that her students are experiencing. Over the week-end, a Snapchat post went out from a student who is not of the Asian diaspora declaring that those Karen people just need to go back where they came from. The post caused significant disruption in the school community. Parents—Karen and others alike—are demanding that the student be expelled.*

Details

*Yanil was assigned a district mentor who is male and serves in a predominately affluent community with just a handful of recent immigrants. Yanil contacted her mentor and asked for time to process the tinderbox situation. After asking Yanil a few questions, he was surprised that she was taking this situation so personally and asked if he could just give her some sound advice. With Yanil's permission, he told her to just follow the response by the policy and keep her board members up to date. He added that speaking with parents would only make the situation worse. Yanil left the mentoring conversation not feeling heard and quite confused, as her discernment/ gut instinct was telling her something else. Yet, this person had been a superintendent for nearly 2 decades, how could he be wrong she wondered.*

*Referring to Table 6.1, the first step a coach/mentor must take toward building meaningful relationships and rapport is to truly get to know the person they are coaching or what The Tools of Cultural Proficiency conceptual framework names as assessing cultural knowledge. Understanding a mentee's background, beliefs, values, and assumptions requires a mindful conversation*

*(Dilts, 1994). A mentor takes time to delve into what brings their mentee into the leadership position they hold and as demanding as it is, what motivates them to continue with their work. Had Yanil's mentor taken time to do this, he may have understood why she was looking at the situation so personally. He could have seen and heard the exceptional strength she holds as a leader of this district and indeed for that moment in time. Possessing a sound understanding of Yanil's worldview and values may have helped him craft questions that facilitated her thinking and allowed her to harness her personal and professional capabilities, ultimately honoring her professional and personal dignity.*

**Reflect on the first time you were partnered with a mentee. What do you remember about the person—their beliefs, values, or personal background? In what ways, if any, did you use this information to guide your mentoring conversations? Without the information, how did the conversation go?**

_______________________________________________________________

_______________________________________________________________

_______________________________________________________________

_______________________________________________________________

Our fast-paced work environment may lead us to think that there is less time to build a strong relationship, and we must get to the work at hand. Also, male mentors may not feel comfortable taking the time to get to know a female mentee at that level for fear of misinterpretation and possible harassment claims. Following the #MeToo movement, fewer males reached out to female employees for mentoring opportunities, either formal or informal (Gebhardt, 2019). Given that men continue to hold 76 percent of the c-suite roles in the K–12 education system, a greater sense of urgency exists for the need to develop strong cross-cultural mentoring skills.

As we continue to analyze this vignette, what role might gender have played in the mentoring experience? Research suggests that gender plays a role in how leaders work to solve work problems and respond to crises (Smith, 2022). What underlying values, beliefs, and assumptions might exist for Yanil? For her mentor?

## A MENTORS TOOLKIT: THE IMPORTANCE OF QUESTIONS

When a mentor seeks to expand their skills and coaching craft to become increasingly culturally proficient, she should be prepared to develop breakthrough questions (Lindsey et al., 2020). These questions are designed to mediate thinking that is open, broad, and possibilities oriented. Breakthrough questions are curated with curiosity as the key ingredient. As discussed earlier, the need for authenticity is paramount, as it moves the mentor to empathetically focus on the needs of the mentee and not any conscious or unconscious direction they believe the mentee should go. Table 6.1 from *Culturally Proficient Coaching* (Lindsey et al., 2020) provides a look into breakthrough curiosity.

**Table 6.1** • *Barriers TO Thinking—Breakthroughs FOR Thinking*

| Barrier Comment/ Question | Essential Element | Breakthrough Question |
|---|---|---|
| *I'm not feeling good about my upcoming interview. That district is all about diversity and equity. I'm afraid I won't know what to say.* | Valuing equity | *Given your experiences with the equity committee, in what ways might you demonstrate your deeply held values for equity during your interview?* |
| *I'm new to the area and new to my job as an assistant supt. The district wanted to bring in new perspectives from outside the district. I guess I'm unsure where to begin.* | Assessing cultural knowledge | *Given some successful experiences from your former district, what might be some assessment strategies you could use to reach out to the new community you serve?* |
| *As a gay, African American, female superintendent, I want to be attentive to all -isms and guarantee policies are in place to ensure all students are in a safe learning environment.* | Manage the dynamics of diversity<br><br>Value of diversity | *You are confident of your public identity and have no need to defend who you are. How might you manage your awareness of your intersectionality (race, gender, sexual orientation),* |

| Barrier Comment/ Question | Essential Element | Breakthrough Question |
|---|---|---|
| *However, giving too much attention to our LGBTQ+ community may bring attention to me, and that becomes a distraction to the work. For example, our board meetings have become disruptive, church members targeting me for how I live. So, I'm stuck. Do I continue to support our programs or just be quiet?* | | *to demonstrate the depth and value of your knowledge of cultural competence to the success of stakeholders?* |
| *I'm confused about where I want to go from here. I've been a director of assessment and instruction for 4 years, and I enjoy what I do. I think I've lost sight of my goal of being superintendent in this district. I don't even know what my next steps should be. I work so hard all the time, I guess I've lost my sense of professional growth.* | Assessing diversity<br><br>Adapt to diversity | *What haven't you thought of yet about different ways of expressing your opinions and experiences that will enable you to manage and maintain your professional growth goals?* |
| ***To the reader:*** **What's a barrier question that's getting in your way?**<br><br>_______________<br>_______________<br>_______________<br>_______________<br>_______________ | ***To the reader:*** **What essential element will shape the action you take?**<br><br>_______________<br>_______________<br>_______________<br>_______________<br>_______________ | ***To the reader:*** **What might be a breakthrough question to open your thinking?**<br><br>_______________<br>_______________<br>_______________<br>_______________<br>_______________ |

## CHARACTERISTICS OF CULTURALLY PROFICIENT BREAKTHROUGH QUESTIONS FOR MENTORS

Breakthrough questions encourage time to think (Lindsey et al., 2020). By asking these thinking questions, the mentor allows new possibilities to surface for the mentee. Effective, culturally proficient breakthrough questions have the following characteristics:

- Consistently take into consideration the difference related to the mentee's identity that may be at play

- Use the essence of one or more Essential Elements for Cultural Proficiency to shape the action in the question

- Use exploratory, plural, and inclusive language

- Use positive intentionality

- Use language to mediate thinking and/or action toward goals

- Use language that redirects thinking from certainty and predictability to curiosity and possibility

Using the characteristics of culturally proficient breakthrough questions, the following are a few examples for a mentor to use in conversation with a mentee:

- *In what ways might you demonstrate your deeply held value for equity during your upcoming interview?*

- *What might be some different assessment strategies you could use as you get to know the community you serve?*

- *How might you utilize and express the intersectionality of who you are to show your knowledge of cultural competence?*

- *What haven't you thought of yet about different ways of expressing your opinions and experiences that will enable you to manage and maintain your professional growth goals?*

How might the characteristics of breakthrough questions and Table 6.1 guide Yanil's thinking? What might be a breakthrough question you would craft if you were her mentor?

_______________________________________________

_______________________________________________

_______________________________________________

_______________________________________________

_______________________________________________

## BENCHMARKING FOR SUCCESS

So how will a mentor know they are successfully transforming their practice in a way that fosters the success of female leaders? Referring to breakthrough characteristics, what questions might mediate personal thinking? The ultimate goal of coaching within a mentoring conversation is to support confidence, clarity, and independence. The authentic relationship recognizes and honors the dignity of the female mentee and uses that background knowledge to support her shift in thinking and behavioral transformation. A measure of success for the mentor is when the mentee responds similar to as follows:

- ▸ "Oh, what a great question! I haven't thought about using my personal story as part of my interview. Let me think more about that."

- ▸ "Hmmm, I've been wondering about that for a while. I'm glad you asked that question. Here's my best thinking, so far. But I know I want to know more."

- ▸ "So . . . Let me think about that. Oh my, that helps me think more about who I am and how that relates to my career goals."

Self-assessing, self-monitoring, and self-directing skills are ways to plan for your growth as a culturally proficient mentor. As we promised in the opening paragraph of this chapter, the mentee who is skilled in asking breakthrough questions knows what to ask for from her mentor. *As we have this time together today, what might be some questions to help me focus on my upcoming interview?* Or, a new faculty member might ask her mentor, *What might be some questions you could ask me to open my thinking to "why aren't there more females in this department"?*

Breakthrough questions use the Essential Elements for Cultural Proficiency to help shift thinking from

- ▸ Being stuck to transformative action
- ▸ Where she is to where she wants to be
- ▸ Certainty to curiosity
- ▸ Current reality to desired outcomes

As you reflect on this chapter, what might be your personal and professional next step(s) toward becoming a culturally proficient mentor?

_______________________________________________________________

_______________________________________________________________

_______________________________________________________________

_______________________________________________________________

Chapter 7 offers our final thoughts and invitation to stay in touch. We want to hear your mentoring story. What might be some insights from reading this book you'll share with others?

# RESOURCES FOR MENTEES AND MENTORS

*A mentor empowers a person to see a possible future, and believe it can be obtained.*

Unknown

## RESOURCES AND STRATEGIES

In a 2023 Forbes article (Phillips, 2023), Dr. Susan Enfield, at that time superintendent of Washoe County Schools, Nevada's second largest school district, reflected specific and broadly shared experiences of so many women in their careers. One of her favorite reflections was the role of other women who supported her. Enfield explained,

> *I was fortunate to know women who were committed to enlightening, educating and empowering other women coming into leadership. It's so vital for them to know their worth, to launch them in those leadership roles, so that they're successful long term.*

She concluded,

> *We need more honest conversations about the difference in experience that gender, race, and identity produce. The time to have strong, courageous, compassionate women in the superintendency is now–it's needed today more than ever.*

The journeys of thousands of women in education leadership demonstrate that to get there, women must materially support other women as they develop their careers. Growing their careers means taking action and putting some real *momentum* behind mentoring, sponsorship, and support so that their leadership can persist.

## KEEP MOMENTUM GOING

As we interviewed and listened to women throughout the nation, we heard comments and sentiments in which you may find your own stories and experiences. One young emerging female leader shared that she had never experienced gender inequities in the workplace. Our response was hopeful but also reminiscent of the fact that she stands on the shoulders of female leaders who have paved the way so that the inequities are not repeated and eventually eliminated.

Can you find yourself in the comments we documented below regarding barriers and support factors for mentors and mentees?

## BARRIERS THAT HAVE GOTTEN IN THE WAY AS A MENTOR

- ▶ My male mentors are much quicker to give advice that aligns with their reality. My female mentors are much more cautious and understand my realities.

- ▶ A male mentor told me that I let my emotions get in the way and I was not ready to mentor other women.

- ▶ My male mentor told me that women have difficulty serving in urban school districts.

- ▶ I have found other female leaders to be barriers. They seem to think there is only one crown to go around.

- ▶ A male coworker often interrupts me when I am talking with my mentee. He oversteps and feels his guidance is better than mine.

## BARRIERS THAT HAVE GOTTEN IN THE WAY AS A MENTEE

- ▶ My mentee is fearful of advancement and how that may impact her personal relationships.

- ▶ My mentee is often overwhelmed, stressed out, and out of balance. She is balancing the roles of leader, wife, and mother and often cannot prioritize being mentored.

- ▶ My mentee feels a lack of confidence. She is very capable.

- ▶ My mentee expresses feelings of being perceived as aggressive, instead of assertive and confident.

- She often cancels because she is too busy, too tired, too overwhelmed. Time for mentoring is not a priority.

- She feels that she is not enough and cannot overcome the "way it's always been" dominance.

- She is not sure how to move up the ladder and balance a family. She wants to do both and questions if it is possible.

- She feels that she is not heard. She offers an idea, and credit is given to her male counterpart. Everyone acts like it is the first time it has been suggested, and the concept is embraced with undue credit to the male.

## SUPPORT FACTORS THAT HAVE MATTERED FOR MENTORS AND MENTEES

- Visible female role models in action

- Supportive mentoring networks

- Strong female superintendent/supervisor who provides opportunities for mentoring programs

- Cognitive coaching participation to improve your mentoring skills

- Conferences, forums, and workshops to promote and learn about the unique contributions of women in leadership

- Sister circles

## ACTIONS TO TAKE

- Join Leading While Female Facebook page.

- Prioritize time for mentoring.

- Tap women on the shoulders, lift them, and let them know of opportunities in leadership.

- Conduct and participate in mock interviews and reviewing resumes with other women.

- Join online and in-person networks designed for women in leadership.

- Reach out and offer to mentor.

- Take the hand of those who offer to mentor.

- Be assertive: find a woman that is or has been successful in your role and ask her to be your mentor.

- Have a regularly scheduled specific time and place outside of the district to meet and confer with your mentor/mentee.

- Support a call, if needed, in between formal meetings.

- Use breakthrough questions similar to the ones listed in this chapter to facilitate deep dialogue between mentor and mentee.

- When the mentoring relationship ends, keep in touch, reach out periodically, and offer friendship.

Did you find yourself in the narrative? Are there questions that you may ask of yourself or others to continue the dialogue and strengthen the support? We offer a few questions to ponder and to share in your networks of women to inspire, motivate, and promote deep and meaningful dialogue.

1. What is one thing that you allowed to happen this year, that you should have stopped? What support do you need to stop it this year?

   a. A female superintendent shared that she is often called "kiddo" by a male colleague in her organization. She is bothered by it and finds it to be disrespectful and patriarchal, yet she does not want to hurt his feelings and has let it continue. She outlined a plan for how to speak with him about this without alienating him or embarrassing him. Addressing this issue will honor her rightful opinion to a perhaps well intended, yet ill received pattern of addressing her.

2. Who will you mentor with additional intention this year?

   a. Seek out a female who is in a role in which you have been or currently are successful and offer a hand up. Perhaps this is a formal offer, or perhaps it is a call if you need me, but the offer will be appreciated and give permission and confidence to the mentee to begin the relationship.

3. What advice do you give to young women aspiring to leadership roles?

   a. Find meaningful moments in your career and generously share them with aspiring leaders. Stacie tells the story of the kindergarten child of color, who looked up at her and said,

"You are Brown. Are you smart?" What a moment in time to memorialize and share with others in her heartfelt, confident, and assuring response to a child who was listening, watching, and learning.

4. How has being a woman influenced your leadership style?

   a. What aspects of being a female are often confused as a weakness but are clearly your greatest strengths? Trudy recalls the time someone confronted her by questioning her strength and said, "I heard you cried today." Her response was a very simple, "thank you." No explanation nor defense was necessary.

5. Tell of a time you experienced a barrier, resistance, or bias based on your gender. How did you handle it?

   a. The telling of our own stories is one of our greatest strengths. May we share those stories freely in order to reduce, minimize, and eventually eliminate the occurrences of gender bias in the workplace.

6. How have you navigated the imposter syndrome?

   a. We all have a right to be here. We have earned that right through our past successes, academic preparation, and life/work experiences, yet we often question if we belong. As women we can assure each other on a consistent basis that we deserve to have not just a seat at the table but a voice at the table. Belonging is not giving up who we are or limiting who we will become.

7. How do you take care of yourself and stay balanced?

   a. As per our discussion in Chapter 4, balance is not something we can all achieve all the time. We need support, and we need to be able to give ourselves grace to say no, cast aside perfectionism, rely on others, and know that we are doing our best. Perhaps the term of work/life blending is a more accurate description of our desire to be effective in our many roles as women who lead in our professions and our personal lives.

8. What woman in your current or previous workplace has inspired you?

   a. Share the qualities of the woman who immediately enters your mind when posed with this question. Was she kind? Was she consistent? Was she courageous? Was she generous? Was she a trail blazer? Was she smart? Was she an excellent communicator? Who was she, and how can we learn from her?

9. What are your future goals and ambitions?

    a. Say it out loud! It will become real if you begin to speak about your goals. A female director in business and finance announced to a Leading While Female network in her district that she had goals to become a chief business official or assistant superintendent of business services. She announced it with an apology and said she did not have the academic preparation, and she was talking about the "future, future, future." Her colleagues jumped in to remind her that her on-the-job performance was exemplary. She did not need academic training and to limit the word "future" to one not three! She said it out loud, and it will become a reality.

10. What do you wish someone had told you when you began your career?

    a. This is an important question as it reminds those of us who are doing the work to share with our emerging sister leaders what they may expect. It also reminds us that we have a role to ensure that a new female joining the leadership team will be much more successful if she can rely on those of us who have led successfully.

11. What is the best way for a woman to negotiate her contract?

    a. If you are in a role where you have an obligation to negotiate your compensation or contract, this may be time to garner assistance through legal counsel, administrative associations, or a mentor who has experience. Know the value of your worth and unapologetically seek assistance to ensure that any compensation is comparable to past, current, and future comparisons of male leaders.

12. What are you most proud of as a woman who leads?

    a. Be proud of your accomplishments, and share them with others. As we learn the accomplishments and the pride of others, we can expand on those sources of pride in our own leadership. As we share dialogue such as this in our networks and forums, we begin to normalize the pride of our accomplishments. This is not boastful. This is hopeful.

We hope that you will use these prompts in your own circles. Each question is designed to remind us of our power and our unique contributions to leadership. We all have much to learn, and we all have much to teach.

As we close, may we remind you that mentoring is an ongoing process. It is not an event. As opportunities come to you, we invite and, in some cases, remind you of the following:

## SHOW APPRECIATION

### Thank You, My Mentor!

Have you sent your mentor a thank you message recently?

When should you send a thank you?

- **Anytime**. Send a hand-written thank you message by regular mail. Email works, also. Text is immediate. Be specific and genuine for what you are grateful.

- **After a special event** that she advised you, let her know how things went and how her words guided you in your role.

- **Following an impactful reflection**, send her your thoughts:
  - Center the context for her because she probably has many mentees.
  - Describe the impact your reflective thinking has had on you.
  - Detail your appreciation of the influence she has had on you, personally and professionally.

Close with contact information and an invitation for a future (even if final) gathering.

### Thank You, My Mentee!

Your mentee decides when she no longer needs your guidance as a mentor. She may bring this relationship to close in a formal or more casual way. Irrespective of her closing, as mentors we can acknowledge and enhance the relationship at any time by showing our appreciation of the mentee.

Have you sent your mentee a *thank you* message recently?

When should you send a thank you?

- **Anytime**. Handwritten notes model your value for time and for her.

- **After a special event** you advised her went well, remind her you saw or heard the success of the event and could see the importance of her role.

- **Following an impactful reflection**, model the importance of reflection and share your "lessons learned."

You are thanking her for the opportunity to grow professionally and personally. Send words of appreciation and encouragement and include contact information for future engagement if she chooses.

## LEGACY MENTORING

How many people have you mentored? Did you keep count over the years? How many people mentored you? Did you keep mentoring journals or stories (no names, please) that you share with other mentees along the way? As superintendents, district office administrators, principals, and educational professors retire from institutions yet look for ways to remain active in the profession, mentoring might be the obvious choice. While sometimes sharing struggling stories with emerging leaders seems appropriate, mentoring is more about developing a professional skill set of ways to share knowledge, experience, and deeply held values with an emerging leader. A mentor builds a trusting relationship with her mentee and provides guidance and support for the mentee to develop equitable leadership skills, align actions with values, and know her why.

Legacy mentoring is choosing to mentor for as long as emerging leaders, or senior leaders, request their services. Legacy mentors are often available to superintendents or executive leaders in organizations. They are also available for peer-to-peer mentoring when a colleague requests a retired member of the profession to serve as her mentor even though they are near the same age. Legacy mentoring simply means much is yet to be shared with our colleagues who are new to *Leading While Female.*

## INFORMAL YET POWERFUL MENTORING

Mentoring is not always formal. Informal mentoring can be an organic process that was not planned but can provide significant opportunities and encouragement. Informal mentors can advocate and sponsor other women as they introduce their colleague to contacts and connections. This sponsorship can be life altering.

Trudy experienced this as she worked in the State of Wisconsin. Upon her departure, she received numerous requests from Wisconsin and neighboring states to speak on the barriers and contributions of Leading While Female. Each time, she asked where they got her contact information, the response was always the same female leader, "Gail from Wisconsin." Gail's involvement and intentional sponsoring was career altering for Trudy as she received open doors from Wisconsin and beyond. Gail modeled the way. Let's follow her lead!

## OUR FINAL THOUGHTS

And so, we come to the closing of this book but certainly not the end of our thinking about mentoring. We leave this book open to our readers for comments and continued thinking about possibilities for mentoring those female leaders who send an invitation for engaging in their future. Women continue to share with us their personal stories of leading and mentoring. We want to hear your *Leading While Female* story here. Use this QR code to share barriers you have overcome, your success story, or your mentor/ mentee story. Your stories are important to us and serve as support factors for others as they are *Leading While Female*.

https://qrs.ly/l2h1g9g

# BOOK STUDY GUIDE FOR
# *LEADING WHILE FEMALE*

Women Mentoring Women for Momentum

**We recommend using this Book Study Guide in the following ways:**

- **Mentoring network book study session**
- **After-school book study sessions**
- **Regional organization book study**
- **Mentoring program book study session**
- **Professional learning book study sessions**
- **Individual mentor skills review**

## BOOK STUDY GUIDE

### Introduction

What struck you about the authors? In what ways do their stories resonate with your mentoring story?

Why did they write this book?

Why might this book stand out as an important book for women mentoring and leading women?

Content Questions to Consider

- What is your mentor story?
- How has your gender formed your narrative as a mentor?
- In what ways have the authors' stories assisted you in reflecting on your own story?
- Who are your mentors?
- Who do you mentor?
- What do you hope for in a mentor?

Personal Reaction Questions to Consider

- What is your reaction to the intent of the book?
- What might be some feelings that surfaced for you as you read the front matter of the book?

## CHAPTER 1: FINDING OUR MOMENTUM

Content Questions to Consider

- What does mentoring for momentum mean to you?
- In what ways did the Terms in Context support your learning?
- How do the exhibits support your learning about the relationships among coaching, mentoring, and sponsoring?

Personal Reaction Questions to Consider

- What was your reaction/response to Delina's story?
- What mentoring experiences have you had as a mentee or mentor?
- What worked for you? What did not work for you?
- Examine your responses to the reflection prompts. What else might you add?

## CHAPTER 2: GROUPS FOR GOOD

Content Questions to Consider

- What strengths do you bring as a mentor?
- What are your areas of continued growth in which you would benefit from a mentor?

Personal Reaction Questions to Consider

- In what environments do you find psychological safety?
- When you feel lonely in the workplace, can you identify the factors that make it feel lonely or exclusive?
- Do you have personal experiences that could add to the richness of the stories of Groups for Good?
- Examine your responses to the reflection prompts. What else might you add?

## CHAPTER 3: EQUITABLE MENTORING MATTERS

Content Questions to Consider

- In what ways do The Tools of Cultural Proficiency inform the work of an equitable mentor?

- What are some of the barriers that get in the way of being an equitable mentor?

- What might be some ways to counter those barriers?

- In what ways did the Continuum for Assessing Growth inform your learning and work as an equitable mentor?

- How do the five Essential Elements provide for momentum for women mentoring women?

Personal Reaction Questions to Consider

- What are your reactions to being an equitable mentor?

- What responses and deeper feelings did you have as you explored the Continuum for Assessing Growth?

- Examine your responses to the reflection prompts. What else might you add?

## CHAPTER 4: PERSONAL AND PROFESSIONAL BLENDING

Content Questions to Consider

- What are your strategies for blending your personal and professional life?

- What is your number one barrier to being a mentor or a mentee?

- How do you handle the barrier of time?

Personal Reaction Questions to Consider

- Which stories about time resonate with you? Do you have a story to share about juggling and the passing of time?

- Do you ever have to give up an aspect of your identity to connect, succeed, or belong in the organization?

- What does your organization have in place to ensure that women participate in mentoring relationships?

- Examine your responses to the reflection prompts. What else might you add?

## CHAPTER 5: WHAT'S MY ROLE?: ROLES, RESPONSIBILITIES, AND RELATIONSHIPS

Content Questions to Consider

- What are the typical roles of the mentee and mentor, and why is it important/critical to know these roles?

- In what ways do networks function to support the role of mentor?

- In what ways do networks function to support the role of mentee?

- What are the purpose(s) of mentor programs, and how might they serve both mentor and mentee to achieve their goals?

- In what ways do stories support mentors' growth?

Personal Reaction Questions to Consider

- What were some emotional connections for you in this chapter?

- How might the barriers inform your mentor story?

- Examine your responses to the reflection prompts. What else might you add?

## CHAPTER 6: BREAKING THROUGH THE MOMENTUM

Content Questions to Consider

- In what ways might coaching skills enhance mentor/mentee relationships?

- How might the Essential Elements of Cultural Proficiency shape breakthrough questions (BTQs)?

- In what ways might BTQs assist mentors in moving their mentees from where they are to where they want to be?

Personal Reaction Questions to Consider

- How are you feeling about the craft of coaching supporting your relationship with your mentees?

- What might be some underlying barriers that get in the way of your relationship with a mentee?

- Examine your responses to the reflection prompts. What else might you add?

## CHAPTER 7: RESOURCES FOR MENTEES AND MENTORS

Content Questions to Consider

- What were your reactions to the barriers as the role of mentor?

- What were your reactions to the barriers as the role of mentee?

- What were your reactions to the support factors for overcoming barriers?

- What will it take to keep the momentum going?

- What's your impression of legacy mentoring?

Personal Reaction Questions to Consider

- Overall, what's your feeling about being a stronger mentor now that you've read this book?

- What is the strength of this chapter that will guide you to keep the momentum going as a mentor?

- In what ways did your personal reaction to this book surprise you?

- Examine your responses to the reflection prompts. What else might you add?

# REFERENCES

AASA: The School Superintendents Association. (2024, December 1). Tenure in the role [Infographic]. *School Administrator Magazine.* https://www.aasa.org/resources/resource/tenure-in-the-role

AAUW. (n.d.) *Fast facts: Occupational segregation.* https://www.aauw.org/resources/article/occupational-segregation/

Arriaga, Trudy T., Stanley, L., & Lindsey, Delores, B. (2020). *Leading while female: A Culturally proficient response for gender equity.* Corwin.

Burns, Kelli. (2025): *Gender equity in K-12 educational leadership,* [Unpublished Doctoral Dissertation]. Cal Lutheran University.

Cobb, Floyd, & Krownapple, John J. (2019). *Belonging through a culture of dignity: The keys to successful equity implementation.* Mimi & Todd Press.

Costa, Arthur, & Garmston, Robert. (1994). *Cognitive coaching: A foundation for renaissance schools.* Christopher-Gordon.

Crenshaw, Kimberle. (2016). *The urgency of intersectionality* [Video]. YouTube. https://www.youtube.com/watch? v=akOe5-UsQ2o

Davila, Jennifer, & Gotian, Ruth. (2023). Tormentor mentors, and how to survive them. *Nature, 16.*dol:10.1038/d41586-023-00821-8, Epub ahead of print. PMID: 36928402.

Delpit, Lisa. (1988). The silences dialogue: Power and pedagogy in educating other peoples' children. *Harvard Educational Review, 58*(3), 280-298.

Dilts, Robert. (1994). *Effective presentation skills.* Capitola.

The History of Coaching: Doctors Who Coach Doctors. (2024). *LinkedIn.* https://www.linkedin.com/pulse/history-coaching-doctors-who-coach-doctors-n0kdc/

The Education Trust. (2023). *Leading with excellence video series.* https://edtrust.org/rti/leading-with-equity-video-series/

Ellingrud, Kweilin, Yee, Lareina, & Martinez, Maria Del Mar. (2024). *The broken rung: When the career ladder breaks for women—and how they can succeed in spite of it.* Harvard Business Review Press.

Gebhardt, Jillesa. (2019). *Men continue to pull back from interacting with women in the wake of #MeToo.* https://www.surveymonkey.com/newsroom/men-continue-to-pull-back-in-wake-of-metoo/

Grogan, M., & Nash, A. M. (2021). Superintendents and the intersections of race, gender and district composition. In C. H. Tienken (Ed.), *The American superintendent 2020 decennial study* (pp. 19-28). Rowman & Littlefield Education.

Hargreaves, Andrew, & Fullan, Michael. (2013). The power of professional capital. *Learning Forward, 34*(3), 36-39.

Higgins, Monica, & Kram, Kathy. (2001), Reconceptualizing mentoring at work: A developmental network perspective. *The Academy of Management Review, 26*(2), 264-288. Academy of Management. http://www.jstor.org/stable/259122

Kram, Kathryn. (1985). *Mentoring at work: Developmental relationships in organizational life.* Scott, Foresman & Company.

Kramer, Andie. (2021, July 14). Women need mentors now more than ever. *Forbes.*

https://www.forbes.com/sites/andiekramer/2021/07/14/women-need-mentors-now-more-than ever/

Lambert, D. (2025). *More women are now leading U.S. school districts, study says.* EdSource. https://edsource.org/updates/more-women-are-now-leading-u-s-school-districts#0

LeaderFactor. (2025). *Four stages of psychological safety.* https://www.leaderfactor.com/learn/four-stages-of-psychological-safety

Leadership Alliance. (2024). *What is a mentor?* https://theleadershipalliance.org/resource/what-mentor).

Lindsey, Delores, Martinez, Richard, Lindsey, Randall, & Myatt, Kieth. (2007). *Culturally proficient coaching: Supporting educators to create equitable schools.* Corwin.

Lindsey, Delores, Martinez, Richard, Lindsey, Randall, & Myatt, Kieth. (2020). *Culturally proficient coaching: Supporting educators to create equitable schools.* Corwin.

Lindsey, Delores, Thousand, Jacqueline, Jew, Cynthia, & Piowlski, Lori. (2018). *Culturally proficient inclusive schools: All means all.* Corwin.

Lindsey, Randall, Nuri-Robins, Kikanza, Terrell, Raymond D., & Lindsey, Delores. (2019). *Cultural proficiency: A manual for school leaders.* Corwin.

Malone, J. (2022, February 1). The power of affinity groups: Fostering belonging at your nonprofit. *TechSoup Blog.* https://blog.techsoup.org/posts/the-power-of-affinity-groups-fostering-belonging-at-your-nonprofit

Maranto, Robert, Carroll, Kristen, Cheng, Albert, & Teodoro, Manuel. (2018). Boys will be superintendents: School leadership as a gendered profession. *Phi Delta Kappa The Professional Journal for Educators.*

McKinsey & Company. (2024). *Women CEO's in America, 2024 Report. Executive Summary.* https://www.mckinsey.com/featured-insights/diversity-and-inclusion/women-in-the-workplace

Mentoring Complete. (2025) (Blog). *Mentoring for global diversity: Navigating cross-cultural dynamics* [Blog]. https://www.mentoringcomplete.com/mentoring-for-global-diversity-navigating-cross-cultural-dynamics/

O'Connor, Rachael, Barraclough, Lauren, & Gleadall, Steven, & Walker, Lucinder. (2024). Institutional reverse mentoring: Bridging the student/leadership gap. British *Educational Research Journal, 51*(1), 344-368, 09 October 2024. https://doi.org/10.1002/berj.4078

Phillips, Vicki. (2023, March 30). The Power of momentum mentoring for women in educational leadership. *Forbes.* https://www.forbes.com/sites/vickiphillips/2023/03/30/the-power-of-momentum-mentoring-for-women-in-education-leadership/

Razzetti, Gustavo. (2018).) The best way to find balance in your life. *Psychology Today.* https://www.psychologytoday.com/us/blog/the-adaptive-mind/201809/the-best-way-find-balance-in-your-life?msockid=01a2facb0ed2695c1095ec6c0f7a68e0

Sawchuk, Stephen. (2022). Why aren't there more women superintendents? *Education Week.* https://www.edweek.org/leadership/why-arent-there-more-women-superintendents/2022/03

Smith, Jessica. (2022). Representation in times of crisis: Women's executive presence and gender-sensitive policy responses to crises. *Journal of European Public Policy, 30*(10), 1984–2009. https://doi.org/10.1080/13501763.2022.2110142

Superville, Denisa. (2022). The revolving door of superintendents: What it looks like in the nation's big districts. *EducationWeek.* https://www.edweek.org/leadership/

the-revolving-door-of-superintendents-what-it-looks-like-in-the-nations-big-districts/2022/12

ThomasFisk, Cory. (2024). Navigating the challenges of being the only woman in the room. *LinkedIn*. https://www.linkedin.com/pulse/navigating-challenges-being-only-woman-room-cm-training-expert--tyfkc/

UCLA.(n.d.). *Program Profile report: Educational leadership program.* https://grad.ucla.edu/requirements/?app=statistics&major=0659

Wallace, Teresa. (2014). Increasing the proportion of female superintendents in the 21st century. *Advancing Women in Leadership, 34*, 48-53.

Watson, T. N., Hodgins, D. W., & Brooks, J. S. (2017). Paradigm shift or paradigm stasis? An analysis of research on U.S. women in educational leadership from 1980 to 2004. *Racially and Ethnically Diverse Women Leading Education: A Worldview Advances in Educational Administration, 25*, 1-22. doi:10.1108/S1479-366020160000025001.

# INDEX

# Free professional learning from leading education experts

 **Live and on-demand webinars**

Get a certificate for PD hours!

 **Videos**

 Podcasts

 Study guides

 **New teacher toolkit**

 **Lessons and strategies**

 **Checklists and assessments**

 **Plain language summaries of education research**

 Book excerpts

 **Other downloadables**

 Blogs

**Leave a review!**
If you enjoyed this book, let us know by leaving a review on **GoodReads.com** or **Amazon.com**.

corwin.com/resources

# CORWIN

**To help every educator
help every student**

We believe | that every single student
deserves a great education

We believe | that knowing our impact is both
a privilege and a responsibility

We believe | that a fair, stable, and thriving
society is built on education